I0821976

LIVING WITHOUT HYPOCRISY

Spiritual Counsels of the Holy Elders of Optina

Archimandrite George (Schaefer), translator

Holy Trinity Publications
The Printshop of St Job of Pochaev
Holy Trinity Monastery
Jordanville, New York

Printed with the blessing of Metroplitan Laurus,
of Eastern America and New York,
First Hierarch of the Russian Orthodox Church
Outside of Russia

Living Without Hypocrisy:
Spiritual Counsels of the Holy Elders of Optina

HOLY TRINITY PUBLICATIONS
The Printshop of St Job of Pochaev
Holy Trinity Monastery
1407 Robinson Road
Jordanville, New York 13361-0036
holytrinitypublications.com

Reprint 2025

ISBN: 978-0-88465-092-8 (hardback)
ISBN: 978-0-88465-368-4 (ePub)

Printed in the United States of America.
Books International, 22883 Quicksilver Dr, Dulles, VA, 20166
booksintl.com

One must unhypocritically live, and to all an example give; then will our work be sure, otherwise it will turn out poor.

St. Ambrose

REVERENCE

One must treat holy books and holy objects with reverence. Above all, one must have fear of God, for it teaches reverence, and it teaches everything good. Careless and irreverent treatment of holy things is a result of habit. This must not happen.

St. Nikon

Perform every work attentively, no matter how unimportant it may seem, as if being done before the face of God. Remember that the Lord sees everything.

St. Nikon

GRACE

The action of grace never leads anyone to despair, but grants the gift of tenderness, joy, long-suffering and spiritual peace.

St. Leo

GIVING THANKS TO GOD

Gratitude in a Christian is such a great thing that, along with love, it accompanies him into the future life, where he will celebrate with them the eternal Pascha.

St. Ambrose

It is disastrous to endlessly grieve and unnecessarily castigate oneself, for we must in all ways thank the Lord for all things, for those punishments with which He may have chastised us in this world.

St. Leo

We must give thanks for all things to the Lord, Who has rightly given us difficulties that we may learn patience, which is more beneficial than comforts, and ennobles the soul.

St. Moses

BLESSING

That which is done with a blessing is greatly pleasing to God, so let us live that every small step of ours is blessed.

St. Anthony

One should not do anything without a blessing. If lay people seek the advice of a more experienced person in matters that are more or less important, all the more must a monk remain in obedience.

St. Barsanuphius

BLESSEDNESS

There are various degrees of blessedness, depending on the merits of each person: some will be with the Cherubim, others with the Seraphim, and so on, but let us be content to be numbered among the saved.

St. Barsanuphius

THE BATTLE WITH LUST

The passion of lust wars against everyone, and at the toll-houses the demon of lust will boast before all the princes of darkness that he provided hell with more spoils than all the rest. Be patient, and implore Divine help!

St. Anatoly

WEALTH

Wealth consists not of many possessions, but of a good conscience, which, apart from corruptible wealth, already has its own rewards, for God is mighty and grants us what is needful.

St. Leo

The essence of wealth is not in material things, but what we have within ourselves. No matter how much you give a person, you will not satisfy him.

St. Anatoly

It is a mistake to think that wealth or abundance, or even sufficient means would be beneficial or reassuring. The rich worry even more than the poor and impoverished. Poverty and being in want are closer to humility and to salvation if only the one who is poor does not become fainthearted, but with faith and hope relies on the all-good Providence of God. Until this day the Lord has fed us, and He has the power to do so in the future.

St. Ambrose

Abundance and plenty spoil people. From fat, as they say, even animals go mad.

St. Ambrose

KNOWLEDGE OF GOD

If we strive to cleanse our hearts from the passions, then according to the amount that we have purified ourselves, Divine Grace will open the eyes of our hearts to the vision of the true Light; for as it is written, *Blessed are the pure in heart, for they shall see God* (Matt. 5:8), but only when we perfect ourselves through humility, for through humility the mysteries are revealed.

St. Macarius

The Lord will teach you His ways (Ps. 24:9). So it says in the psalm. God does teach man His ways, but only when that man is meek and humble. God teaches only such people.

St. Nikon

The story of Job is an example for every person. As long as a man is rich, famous, and content, God pays him no mind. When a man is on a dung heap, rejected by everyone, then God appears and converses with him, and the man in return cries out, "Lord have mercy!"

St. Nektary

DIVINE SERVICES

Without the visible Holy Church, there could not be the Holy Mysteries of Christ, without which man could not inherit eternal life. Prayers during church services have so much power and significance that just the words, "Lord, have mercy," surpass all the spiritual exercises performed in one's cell. For this reason the Holy Fathers, while standing in church during divine services, imagined themselves standing before the very throne of God in heaven!

St. Anthony

How good it is to be in church to hear the holy prayers, the chanting, and the psalms! What depths are concealed in the psalms and other sacred prayers! Of course, the reader cannot grasp everything, but if just one thought makes an impression, that is good.

St. Nikon

It is a sin to spend time in idleness. To substitute church services and one's prayer rule with work is also a sin.

St. Ambrose

One should go to the morning services, because during the Divine Liturgy the Bloodless Sacrifice is offered to God on our behalf. By attending the morning services we in turn offer ourselves as a sacrifice to the Lord, we sacrifice our rest for Him.

St. Moses

FORTITUDE OF SPIRIT

Your spirit should not grow weary, but should become warm from spiritual reading, from thoughts about eternity, and from prayer, even though it may be brief. Say to the Lord; "Gather my scattered mind, O Lord and humble my hardened heart with fear of Thee, and have mercy on me!" For without Divine help we are powerless; we cannot even deal with flies, much less invisible enemies.

St. Anthony

GOD'S REWARD

In the depths of His unfathomable wisdom, the Lord does not always fulfill our petitions immediately, but puts them off for some time. However, He does not leave unrewarded anything good done in His name. If he does not reward the mother and father, then He generously rewards their children and descendants, for the Lord is righteous and there is no unrighteousness in Him.

St. Anthony

SICKNESS

We are visited by sicknesses and sorrows. This is an indication of God's mercy towards us, For whom the Lord loveth, He chasteneth, and scourgeth every son whom He receiveth. (Heb. 12:6), and so it is proper for us to thank the Lord for His fatherly Providence for us. Sorrows instruct us and make us skillful in our work, and likewise they, along with sickness, cleanse us of sins.

St. Macarius

We do not know the judgements of God, but He does everything for our benefit. We are bound to earthly blessings, but He desires to give us future blessings through brief sicknesses on this earth.

St. Macarius

When a man acquires a courageous spirit, then in times of all infirmities and physical ailments he can be peaceful and content with his situation.

St. Anthony

What can you do? For the Lord has already established that our temporary life will not pass without sorrows, and it is said, "Always be mindful of your sickness and be sorrowful in your heart." But what is more amazing is that not one holy man, no matter how holy and perfect he may have been, passed his life without having to endure something – and this so that man be not puffed up with pride. And if the saints endured, how much more must we endure!

St. Anthony

Bodily illnesses are sent to man from God not always as punishment for sin, but sometimes through His kindness, for freeing or preserving us from spiritual sicknesses, which are incomparably more dangerous than physical ones.

St. Anthony

Learn to be silent more, and you will not sin and judge others. When you will cease complaining and will zealously care for the sick for God's sake, then you will be freed from your illnesses, not only of the body, but also of the soul. If after your correction the illness does not leave, then it means that for your patience you will be given a crown in the future unending life.

St. Joseph

SPIRITUAL WARFARE

Our life is a spiritual warfare with unseen evil spirits. They arouse us through our passions and urge us to disobey the commandments of God. When we look and investigate carefully, we will find that for every passion there is a cure, a commandment opposing it; and therefore the enemies try to keep us from this saving cure.

St. Macarius

It is impossible to be delivered from the mental wolves without the aid of Christ – His almighty grace is needed to repel them, not the feeble help of man. To obtain this help, a person must throw himself at the feet of Jesus Christ with extreme humility, implore Him for everything, cast all his sorrows on Him, and even more than this, pray to the Mother of God and all the saints with the sincere acknowledgement of his sins and his inability to correct himself.

St. Moses

The struggle with the passions is indispensable; for the darkness and gloom of the passions obscure our spiritual vision, so that we cannot see the Sun of Righteousness, Jesus.

St. Macarius

Struggle against the passions. The warfare with them and the invisible enemies is relentless, terrible, and ferocious. Humility, however, defeats them.

St. Macarius

It is impossible to avoid those spiritual battles, in which we sometimes conquer, and at other times are conquered. If we see that something is not within our power, we should leave it as it is. Wanting to hold on to it or make it more to your liking will only bring harm to yourself, and add sorrow to sorrow.

St. Leo

Whoever overcomes one passion conquers one demon, and whoever overcomes two passions conquers two demons, and whoever forsakes ten or more passions defeats a whole regiment of demons and will enjoy spiritual peace.

St. Anthony

Are you fighting against your passions? Fight, fight, and be good soldiers of Christ! Do not give in to evil and do not be carried away by the weakness of the flesh. During the time of temptation, flee to the Physician, crying out with the Holy Church, our mother: "O God, number me with the thief, the harlot, and the publican (i. e.,with the repentant), and save me!"

St. Anatoly

You should know which of the passions torments you the most, and you should especially struggle against it. To achieve this, you must examine your conscience daily.

St. Nikon

Victory over the passions happens through the power of God. Our feeble powers are not capable of this. We must humbly recognize this and thereby attract the mercy and help of God to ourselves through humility.

St. Nikon

May the Lord give us the wisdom to carry on our battle with the enemy of our salvation and with sin without duplicity; without the wisdom of the Lord and His help, victory is impossible. We are infirm and weak without Divine help, but with the help of God, all things are possible, as the Apostle Paul said: *I can do all things through Christ which strengtheneth me* (Phillip 4:13).

St. Nikon

In the pure writings of the Holy Fathers, we see that he who desires to cleanse his heart of the passions must call on the Lord for help. This is so, but we cannot even say the Jesus Prayer without our thoughts being plundered. With beginners, God does not demand undistracted prayer: it is acquired with much time and labor. As the writings of the Holy Fathers say: "God gives prayer to him who prays," and so we must nevertheless continue to pray, orally, and with the mind.

St. Hilarion

No matter how much the waves of temptation rise up against your soul, always hasten to Christ. The Saviour will always come to your aid and will calm the waves. Believe that the Lord has providentially arranged such experiences for your soul's healing and do not reject them, seeking bodily peace and imaginary tranquility, for it is better to be shaken and yet to endure. If you will gain an insight from this, it will greatly lighten your struggle and you will gain more peace than if you do not.

St. Leo

Do not permit yourself to become greatly confused and despondent due to the fact that the operations of the enemy have started anew both within and without, because they were hidden and lurking within you. But when there unexpectedly came an occasion for your anger and grief to be inflamed, they were revealed and became uncontrollable. In such cases, let us immediately hasten to God, and to our one protectress and defender, the Mediatrix of us all, the most Holy Theotokos and ever-virgin Mary, and She, through Her all-powerful prayers and intercession, will heal all our infirmities, physical and spiritual!

St. Leo

If you will only continue to do your assigned duties and obediences, and will try in every possible way to reveal all of your deeds and all of your thoughts which come from the enemy, the devil, and will strive in all ways to cut off your own will, and in no way believe your own thoughts, will stay far away from doubting and judging others as from a deadly poison, and with the cooperation of grace will struggle to correct yourself, then I daresay that the All-Merciful Saviour will not only heal your wounds, but He will also grant you the gifts of humility and discretion!

St. Leo

Say the Jesus Prayer against lustful temptations, but during temptations of anger, pray for the one who has upset you: "Save, O Lord, and have mercy on ____, and through her holy prayers help me, accursed and sinful."

St. Ambrose

What should someone do who is troubled and disturbed involuntarily by animosity and anger, envy and hatred, or is confused by lack of faith? First of all, one must give full attention to the causes of these passions and then use the appropriate spiritual medicine against those causes. Lack of faith comes from the love of earthly glory, as the Lord Himself affirms in the Holy Gospel: *How can ye believe, which receive glory one of another, and seek not the honour that cometh from God only?* (John, 5:44). But envy, anger, and hatred come from pride and lack of love for one's neighbor.

St. Ambrose

In spring, a gardener first of all clears the ground of all unwanted weeds, and then plants vegetables in clean soil. Soon the weeds come back again, and continue to do so throughout almost the entire summer, and the gardener must carefully weed and clear away all the unwanted plants several times until his crop of vegetables is strong enough to survive. Our body is created from the same earth, and no matter how much a man tries to cleanse himself of the passions, the passions appear again, just like weeds. Let us turn again to the garden which, if it is poorly attended, will suffer damage from goats and swine. Also, birds can fly through fencing. The gardener must be vigilant against all of these enemies and guard his crop. The Christian must guard his spiritual crop from the mental birds, which are sometimes transformed into other beasts. Our Forefather Adam was told: *In the sweat of thy face shalt thou eat thy bread, till thou return unto the ground; for of it was thou taken.* (Gen. 3:19)

St. Ambrose

LOVE OF NEIGHBOR

May the Lord give you the wisdom and the strength to bear one another's burdens and so fulfill the law of Christ, as well as love and peace. May the mistakes, faults and sins of the brethren be mine.

St. Moses

You must bear the spiritual infirmities of your brother gladly, and without annoyance. For when someone is physically ill, we are not only not annoyed with him, but we are exemplary in our care for him; we should also set an example in cases of spiritual illness.

St. Moses

If you must correct or reprimand someone, first pray to God for him in your heart. At times you think that the brother will not accept correction, but if you pray for him first, beyond your expectations you will see that he listens to the reprimand peacefully and indeed corrects himself.

St. Moses

If you want to be spiritually tranquil, never part from someone while feeling agitated, but try in every way to forgive everyone in your soul and to make peace as much as possible, so that you will part with each other in a peaceful spirit, and in this way you will enjoy spiritual peace.

St. Moses

FAITH

Guard the holy faith, that priceless treasure, and with it enter the Kingdom: it is not for something trivial that we labor, but for acquiring a kingdom, and what a kingdom – a heavenly one! We want to be made its citizens.

St. Barsanuphius

There was a wealthy man who became destitute; this was difficult, but it could be overcome. There was a healthy man who became ill, and this too could be remedied, for with the poor and the sick, there is always Christ. However, if you lose your faith, it is a great tragedy. It is truly terrible for such a man, for he has no support.

St. Barsanuphius

A time of trial has now come; do we have faith? A person can maintain his faith who believes fervently and sincerely, to whom God is the dearest of all. Only he who guards himself from every sin can guard his faith, according to the Gospel: *Light is come into the world, and men loved darkness rather than light, because their deeds were evil* (John 3:19).

St. Nikon

There are times when the Lord permits a person to feel as if he has been abandoned, yet He still guards and leads his soul to salvation. This allowance by God can even pertain to an entire group of the faithful. Our primary concern is to preserve the Faith of Christ. If we keep our faith, it is the hope of our salvation. One must guard his faith and avoid every sin.

St. Nikon

I implore you to live piously in order that you might preserve your Orthodox faith, in order that no one and nothing, no circumstances and no kind of sorrow can turn you away from it. For this you absolutely must pray, seeking God's help to keep your faith pure.

St. Nikon

In the Holy Gospel, the Lord Himself says: *Be ye therefore wise as serpents, and harmless as doves* (Matt. 10:16). According to commentaries, the wisdom of the serpent consists of the fact that when a serpent is attacked, it first of all protects its head; similarly, in times of misfortune and difficult circumstances, the Christian must first of all protect his faith. Secondly, the wisdom of the serpent consists of the fact that when it wants to shed its old skin, it slithers into a tight space, otherwise it will not be able to shed his skin. Likewise with the Christian, if he wishes to shed himself of the "old man," he must take the narrow path, according to the Gospel teaching. The harmlessness of the dove consists in gentleness and forgiveness of offenses, vexations, and similar things.

St. Ambrose

A woman cannot live without faith. Either she lives for a period of time without faith and then soon returns to faith in God, or she quickly begins to go to pieces. It is another matter for a man: it is possible for him to live without faith. He hardens completely and becomes a pillar of salt, and so he lives, stiff and cold. But a woman cannot live like this.

St. Barsanuphius

ATTENTION

One must be accurate and attentive in all things. Attentiveness, punctuality and accuracy in all things and in one's duties will even help in your morning spiritual disciplines, when you have become accustomed to being attentive.

St. Barsanuphius

ABSTINENCE

The angels gave glory to God with shepherds. Why was such honor and glory granted to simple shepherds? Because of their simple-heartedness and their simple way of life, which St. John Chrysostom likened to the life of St. John the Forerunner due its severity and deprivations. They barely had a loaf of bread, and drank water from a spring when it was possible. In the psalms it says: *He shall drink of the brook in the way; therefore shall he lift up his head.* (Ps. 109:7.). He who eats rich food and drinks expensive drinks cannot lift up his thoughts on high, but wanders and crawls about on the earth.

St. Ambrose

Practice abstinence according to your strength and turn your attention to interior work: self-rebuke, humility, patience, love; do not reprove your neighbors, and do not judge, look only at your own sins and infirmities.

St. Macarius

Abstinence in moderation is more helpful than anything.

St. Nikon

THE WILL

Not trusting in yourself and not acting according to your own will and understanding is the path to humility; without this, even though we may do good, it is not pleasing to God.

St. Macarius

It is much better to reject your own will and submit. If you do so, in the future all will be good and joyful.

St. Isaaky

THE WILL OF GOD

Do not allow yourself to be to be overly concerned with the judgements of fate. Just have an unwavering desire for salvation and, standing before God, await His assistance until the time comes.

St. Ambrose

If we wholeheartedly rely on the will of God, then everything will be fine, and what is unpleasant will be accepted like as it should be. Everything that happens leads to the salvation of our souls, and in this is revealed great and profound wisdom. *To them that love God, all things work together for good* (Rom. 8:28).

St. Nikon

In this world, nothing is continuous. Look in the street: in the morning there is rain, at noon, it is clear, and in the evening it is cold again. Wind, then calm, cold, then hot; so also in our life. Always be ready to follow the will of God, whether it is pleasing to you or not.

St. Anatoly

At the present time there can be situations in which we cannot just do our own will, but there is no one to turn to and ask. What to do? We must think what our Lord would do in His meekness... The commandments of God were, and always will be, the foundation of life. Entrust yourself to the will of God.

St. Nikon

Before doing anything, pray and think: would this be wise and pleasing to God?

St. Nikon

When one is following the will of God, no insurmountable obstacles will stand in the way.

St. Leo

Having the sincere desire to serve the Lord God and fully entrusting yourself, everything, and everyone to the all-good, perfect will of God bring divine peace to the heart, even when enduring various sorrows, both outward and interior, spiritual ones. Pray to God to be delivered from misfortune and cut off your own will as being sinful and blind. Entrust yourself, your body and soul, your circumstances, both present and future; entrust those close to your heart, and your neighbors to the holy and most wise will of God...Glory be to God! Glory be to God! For all things, glory be to God! Through these wonderful and holy words, the dark thoughts and heaviness will flee. Peace, comfort, and joy then come to the soul of a person. May Thy will be done, O Lord! Glory be to God for all things!

St. Nikon

From the beginning, set out with prayer on the path of salvation, and then you will become a Christian; a meek, silent example, attracting others to this path.

St. Anatoly

Pray like a child, in simplicity of heart, concerning all your needs and sorrows, and entrust yourself to God's will, for the Lord arranges our salvation.

St. Nikon

One must always pray that the Lord will show him the way... Let us pray to the Lord that He will save us and will come to our aid in times of sorrow and need. I see no other refuge or hope. Human solutions are vain and mistaken. When you have to endure something which is very difficult, but you know that it is not of your own will, you receive moral relief and peace of soul. May God's will be done! May the Lord not discredit our faith and devotion to His will. Our only hope is in God. He is our firm foundation, for everything else is unsure. You absolutely do not know where it might be better, where it might be worse, or what to expect. May God's will be done! Our work is to preserve ourselves in the faith, and to keep ourselves from every sin, and entrust everything else to God.

St. Nikon

We must be certain that the Divine Providence of God always watches over us, and arranges all circumstances for our benefit, even when they are unpleasant for us.

St. Leo

Human pride says, "We will make... we will accomplish... we will build a tower at Babel." "We demand of God an account of His actions, for we desire to control the universe, we have dreams of thrones beyond the clouds" --but no one and nothing obeys, and man is proven to be absolutely powerless through his own bitter experience. Through my observation of this in a study of history, in past times, and even in the present, I have come to the conclusion that the ways of Divine Providence are inscrutable to us; we cannot understand them, and therefore it is necessary that we entrust ourselves with all humility to the will of God.

St. Nikon

We must always say: "O Lord, let it be according to Thy will," either this way or that, for we must receive all that is sent to us as from the hand of God; the sorrowful with patience, the pleasant with thanksgiving.

St. Moses

Being able to determine the will of God is possible for those who are pure, by virtue of their way of life. They receive the gift of spiritual discretion, which is higher than all the virtues.

St. Nikon

Christ our Saviour said concerning Himself: *I seek not Mine own will, but the will of the Father that sent Me* (John 5:30). Having in mind the bitter cup of suffering, He knelt down and prayed, saying: *O My Father, if it be possible, let this cup pass from Me; nevertheless, not as I will, but as Thou wilt* (Matt. 26:39). Let us reason in a manner as did Christ Jesus. Gazing at Him, the Source of our faith, let us proceed with patience to our appointed struggle, strengthening ourselves with the humble prayer, "Let it be done unto me, O Lord, according to Thy will!"

St. Moses

If you carefully observe the details of your life and that of others, with startling clarity you will see that no amount of caution or measure taken has ever been able to determine what will transpire, for everything happens according to the judgement of God. There is no one to blame. We must humble ourselves and endure, otherwise we sin against God.

St. Nikon

It would be difficult to exist on this earth if there were no one who could help us to understand life. But you know that the Lord Almighty, Who is over us, is Love itself. Trust in the will of the Lord, and He will not discredit you. Show your trust not with words, but with deeds. Life has become difficult because people have complicated it with their own reasonings, and instead of turning to God for help, they turn to their own understanding and rely solely on it. Do not fear sorrows or sickness or sufferings or any kind of trials, for all of this is a visitation from God and is for your benefit.

St. Anatoly

The merciful Lord accomplishes and does everything through His will for our benefit, even though the means and results may seem to be in opposition to us. With the help of the most Merciful Lord God, we will be patient, and we will see...

St. Leo

The Lord, the Judge, is never hypocritical. In His own time He judges everything righteously, and will reward everyone according to his deeds. Our main endeavor, as long as we remain in this life, is to endure everything, to humble ourselves and to implore the Lord for His help and His mercy, and all will be well.

St. Ambrose

The all-good Providence of God always arranges what is most beneficial for us, while in our ignorance, we very often strive for the very opposite. From time immemorial, the murderer has threatened to commit murder, but it has been said that that hour has not yet come. Only the Lord knows how he will be able to accomplish this crime, or if it will even happen at all. For instance, having entrusted themselves to the will of God, some people died a martyric death, while others, according to God's will, simply died in prison. Let us also entrust ourselves to the will of God and His all-good Providence in order that He might arrange for us what is good and salvific, as He ordains and as it is pleasing to Him.

St. Ambrose

In one place people prayed for rain; in another they prayed for it's cessation. It turned out as God ordained.

St. Ambrose

My child! Submit to the will of God, and the enemy will flee from you, having been shamed by you. Stand where you can in church and say the Jesus Prayer like the Publican, and the Lord will help you.

St. Ambrose

We must entrust everything to the will of God, even our being separated from each other. The Lord enlightens us in order that we not become attached to the things of this world, no matter how precious they might seem, in order that we might strive for the heavenly, saving our souls. Strive only to save your soul, for everything else is vanity. Everything of this world is ephemeral. Our thoughts must be with God, in the future life. Everything of this world will pass.

St. Nikon

FORTUNE TELLING - SORCERY

You do not need fortune tellers; it is better to rely on the will of God. Those who go to fortune tellers are two-faced people who do not hope in the mercy and help of God. They seek the help of men and have more hope in the calculations of men and not in God and His all-powerful help and His all-present Providence.

St. Ambrose

THE EDUCATION OF CHILDREN

The Old Testament says: *A foolish son is a grief to his father, and a bitterness to her that bore him.* (Prov. 17:25), that is, a son who has not been instructed in the fear of God nor in the law of God. At the present time, many parents teach their children many things which ultimately are neither necessary nor beneficial, but take no care in instructing the children in the fear of God, or to fulfill the commandments of God, and to adhere to the teachings of the One, Holy, Cath-

olic and Apostolic Church. Because of this, children, for the most part, are disobedient and disrespectful to their parents, useless to themselves and to their country, and sometimes are even dangerous.

St. Ambrose

One should trace on the soft young heart the Sweetest Name – the radiant prayer: "Lord Jesus Christ, Son of God, have mercy on me a sinner." From that time on there will be the greatest joy and eternal happiness. When Jesus is established in the heart, one will desire "neither Rome nor Jerusalem," for the King Himself, along with His All-hymned Mother and all the angels and saints will themselves come and abide in him. *I and the Father will come unto him, and make our abode with him.* (cf. John 14:23)

St. Anatoly

It will be enough if you take care to instruct your children in the fear of God, instill them with an Orthodox understanding, and by teaching them to be faithful, you protect them from reasoning that is foreign to the teachings of the Orthodox Church. The good that you sow in the hearts of your children while they are young will blossom forth in their hearts when they come to full maturity, after enduring the bitter trials of school and contemporary life, which often break off the branches of a good Christian upbringing in the home.

St. Ambrose

If you succeed in planting the fear of God in the hearts of your children, then the caprice of human behavior will not be able to harm them.

St. Ambrose

Before your child's first confession, take the time to prepare him for this Mystery as much as you can. Before his confession, have your child read about the commandments and what each of them means. Concerning the correction of his shortcomings in general, you can say to him in a half-joking manner, "You are a little prince you know, and if you behave like that, you might get mud on your face!"

St. Ambrose

We are required to teach children, and we must learn from them as well, as the Lord Himself said: *If you will not be as little children, you will not enter the kingdom of heaven.* (Matt. 18:3) The Apostle Paul interprets this line: *Brethren, be not children in understanding: howbeit in malice be children, but in understanding be men.* (I Cor. 14:20)

St. Ambrose

At the appropriate time you can say to your daughter that as a good Christian girl she should read spiritual books, not just magazines, and she must not believe every foolish thing she reads without verifying it, for example, that man can be born from dust, and that man has evolved from monkeys. However, it is true that people have begun to imitate monkeys and have lowered themselves in behavior to the level of monkeys.

St. Ambrose

In preparing your children for life in the world, have you taken care to plant in their hearts faith and the fear of God, which will be their guides in the future? Pray to the Lord that He protect their hearts from the tares which are sown among the wheat by the enemy.

St. Macarius

Give children good instructions in morality, and when they will be worthy, and if it will be beneficial to them, God is powerful to enrich them or give them enough of what they need.

St. Macarius

May God grant that the child will have the character of a little lamb, and not that of a little goat! Lambs are peaceful, quiet, and obedient, while little goats are frisky, jumpy, loud, prone to butting, and for this reason they are pleasing to no one.

St. Anthony

You think that it would be better for your son to be with you all the time, but who knows? With you, if God permits, he could become spoiled, while in the hands of others, preserved from harm. In the end, regardless of where your children might be, with you or in the care of someone else, instill in them Christian principles and entrust them to God and the intercession of the Mother of God.

St. Macarius

ENMITY

Those who are indignant with us teach us to carefully consider and examine ourselves: Are we really Christians? Do we love our enemies? Thus we acknowledge our infirmities.

St. Macarius

SNARES OF THE ENEMY

We are spiritual soldiers, and we have irreconcilable and invisible enemies who are dauntless, most evil, and who endlessly try to conquer and destroy that city which is our soul. We must not continue our life of laziness and sinful slumber, but imploring the help of God, we must stand up against our enemy. He only has power against us when we are confident and become proud of ourselves; but if we conduct ourselves with humility in every situation, then all the snares and power of the enemy are destroyed.

St. Macarius

Our chief enemies are the demons who fight to conquer us through our passions. The most powerful weapon against all their evil machinations, snares and arrows is humility. They are the creatures of pride, and are able to conquer those who proudly think that they can do battle with them; but they cannot stand up against humility.

St. Macarius.

The nets of the enemy are very fine and not easily perceived; only humility can escape them.

St. Macarius

The Gospel says: *Pray for your enemies* (cf. Matt. 5:44); and indeed, desiring to attack us and cause us harm, the enemies act in such a manner exclusively because of their ill-will towards us. Yet, by their malice they actually cut short, for the most part, an even greater harm which threatens us. Therefore they are our actual benefactors for whom we most certainly must pray!

St. Anthony

We should not have visible enemies. There is one weapon against them: praying for them. But we have always had and always will have many invisible enemies.

St. Barsanuphius

The lazy spider sits in one spot, sets out its net, and waits. And as soon as a fly gets caught in the web, right away - off with its head! ...and the fly just buzzes. In like manner, the enemy always spreads his nets; and as soon as someone is caught – off with his head! Take care that you not be like that fly, or you will also be buzzing!

St. Ambrose

TIME

The person who has succeeded in lighting his lamp will rejoice forever with the most sweet and desired Bridegroom in the unceasing company of those who keep festival. This lamp is prayer; the heart is the wick, prayer itself is the flame. The ineffable joy experienced in the prayerful heart is the action of the Holy Spirit, or the bliss in the bridal chamber with the Heavenly Bridegroom. Therefore I exhort and implore you: do not grow sluggish and do not waste precious time in laughter and joking. All these temporary "comforts" will turn into a burning coal, a loathsome stench and an unbearable sorrow, and there will be nowhere to flee. For this reason did our Saviour say to His beloved disciples, *Watch and pray, that ye enter not into temptation.* (Matt. 26:41)

St. Anatoly

ANGER

Recognize the root of anger and wrath: it is pride. Root it out with its very opposite, humility, with the help of God, Who looks upon the humble.

St. Macarius

You become upset and malice against everyone boils in your soul; this is from self-love and vainglory. Always strive to consider yourself to be worse and more sinful than anyone on the earth in the sight of God. During such a time, fervently say, "Lord have mercy on us sinners," which will include you and those with whom you have become angry.

St. Joseph

No one can blame their irritability on this or that illness – it comes from pride. According to the words of the Apostle James, *"The wrath of man worketh not the righteousness of God."* (James 1:20) In order not to give into irritability and anger, you must not hurry.

St. Ambrose

An irritable state of soul comes, first of all, from self-love, when something happens not according to our desire or point of view, and secondly, from lack of faith that fulfilling the commandments of God in the given situation will bring no benefit.

St. Ambrose

If you feel that you cannot control your anger, remain silent, and for the time being say nothing, until, through continuous prayer and self-reproach, your heart has become calm.

St. Hilarion

PERSECUTION

At the present time, people in the world consider us believers to be foolish and stupid. They do not approve of our Orthodox faith, or ecclesiastical rules, laws and customs. They scornfully laugh at everything that is holy to us. You can often hear from believers, who are forced to live in a hostile environment, how difficult it is to endure constant mockery and derision. You should consider such treatment an honor: *If ye be reproached for the name of Christ, happy are ye; for the spirit of glory and of God resteth upon you.* (I Peter 4:14) If people laugh at us, if they do not love us, it means that we are not of this world. We should not be grieved or upset over such treatment.

St. Nikon

Then shall they deliver you up to be afflicted, and shall kill you; and you shall be hated of all nations for My name's sake. (Matt. 24:9) These words refer to all Christians who lived in the first centuries of Christianity, and who will live in the last times of the Church of Christ on this earth.

St. Barsanuphius

Persecution and oppression are beneficial for us, for they strengthen us in our faith.

St. Nikon

PRIDE

All problems come from pride; it is the main source of our sins, distress, and misfortune.

St. Macarius

Where there is a fall, even if only in thought, it was preceded by pride.

St. Macarius

Since we consider ourselves to be debtors before God, we must not flee from reproaches, rebukes, and offenses. Through these, not only is our debt paid off, but that terrible spiritual illness, pride, is healed through the application of these spiritual "plasters," with God's help.

St Leo

Pride, more than anything else, deprives people of both their good deeds and the help of God. Where there is no light, there is darkness, and where there is no humility, pride takes its place.

St. Macarius

The cornerstone of the monastic life is humility. Both humility and obedience help us to acquire a number of virtues, especially in the physical sense; however, if we are proud, all is lost. For example, five hundred ruble notes lose their value if they are thrown into the fire. As long as they are not close to the flames, they retain their great value, but the minute they fall into the fire, they turn into useless ashes, having no value. Similarly, a person who has many virtues, but is proud, is like a great ship laden with an extremely valuable cargo, but not finding a safe harbor sinks into the waters of the ocean. See on the one hand how powerful and destructive is pride, and on the other, how salvific the virtue of humility. *But to this man will I look, even to him, that is poor and of contrite spirit, and trembleth at my word,* says the Lord. (Isaiah 66:2)

St Barsanuphius

Arrogance, or pride, is so destructive that from the heights of the virtues, it casts one down to the abyss of passions and vices.

St. Macarius

Behind pride, and literally in its steps, the sin of fornication always follows.

St. Barsanuphius

Is there a noble pride? No, there is only demonic pride.

St. Moses

If you cannot live with your own sister, it seems that you will not get along with an angel in paradise because of pride.

St. Joseph

God himself heals the proud. This means that inner sorrows (by which pride is cured) are sent to us by God, for the proud man will not suffer anything from others. But the humble person will endure everything, and will always say, "I deserve this."

St. Ambrose.

Pride is at its worst when we ourselves do not notice it. But, if we notice it and are repentant and contrite, the Lord does not count it as a sin.

St. Anatoly

You do not just suddenly leap into heaven, but you enter it with humility. The worst of all sins is when we are overwhelmed by our pride and our own opinion about everything.

St. Macarius

For one who is proud, asking forgiveness is very difficult. Satan also is not capable of this, and hates to ask forgiveness.

St. Anatoly

If you are constantly angry and complaining, it is indicative of a proud soul. Humble yourself, reproach yourself, and the Lord is powerful to give you comfort and a helping hand.

St. Anatoly

SIN

There are those sins which are deadly, and those which are not. A deadly sin is one for which you will go to hell if you die without repenting of it, but if you do repent, it is immediately forgiven. It is called deadly because it causes the death of the soul, and the soul resurrects only through repentance. This sin is to the soul what a mortal wound is to the body. There are those wounds which can be healed and will not cause death to the body, and then there are mortal wounds. Likewise with sins. A grave sin destroys the soul, and renders it unfit for spiritual blessedness. For example, if you sit a blind man at a place with a wonderful view and ask him, "Isn't the view just lovely from here?" Of course, he will have to answer that he can see nothing because he is blind. So it can be said about a soul deadened by sin, which is incapable of eternal blessedness.

St. Barsanuphius

Sin leaves it is mark not only on the soul, but also on the exterior of a person, on his outward appearance and behavior.

St. Nikon

Why do people sin? Either because they have no idea how they should act and what they should avoid, or if they do know, they forget, or if they do not forget, then they become lazy and despondent. Since people are often indolent when it comes to piety, and they very often forget that their main obligation is to serve God, from laziness and not being mindful they progress to complete thoughtlessness and ignorance. Despondency or laziness, forgetfulness, and ignorance are three giants which bind the whole race of mankind in unbreakable bonds, causing indifference towards the hosts of evil passions. For this reason we must pray to the Heavenly Queen: "My Most-Holy Lady Theotokos, through Thy holy and all-powerful prayers, take from me, Thy humble and sinful servant, despondency, forgetfulness, thoughtlessness, carelessness, and all defiled, evil, and blasphemous thoughts..."

St. Ambrose

No one and not one thing can bring harm to a person if he does not harm himself, and conversely, a thousand ways and means to salvation will not help the person who will not avoid sin.

St. Nikon

GIFTS

Do not seek lofty gifts, or spiritual ecstasy and comfort, for they are granted to us according to the measure of our humility. How is it possible for a person to enter the wedding feast of the Royal Bridegroom when he is clothed in the filthy garment of the passions? Let us purify ourselves with repentance and humility, and let us allow the will of God, when it will be pleasing to Him, to lead us into the Bridal Chamber, and let us consider ourselves unworthy of it.

St. Macarius

Although pleasant feelings and tears are sometimes experienced, one should not grant them much attention, considering them to be something great. Instead, you should humble yourself, considering yourself to be unworthy of such gifts. The more lofty the lives of the Holy Fathers, the more they belittled and humbled themselves, and humility attracted to them even more so the gifts and grace of God.

St. Macarius

GOOD WORKS

Avoid evil and do good; at first, out of fear of God, then later you will acquire the love of God.

St. Macarius

Do not forget about humility which must be joined to every good work, and without which any works we might do will bring us no benefit – only harm, which we see happen with many people. Even though you fast, you pray or give alms, beware of the thought that you are doing good. This the enemy tries to present in order to destroy all your fruit and distance your soul from God.

St Macarius

Not every "good" deed is actually good, but only that good deed which is done for the sake of God. The externals of a particular action are not its essence; God alone sees a person's heart. We need to humble ourselves, realizing that every good deed is mixed with some passion.

St. Nikon

We know from the Holy Scriptures that we were not just created to eat what tastes good to us, to live a pleasant life. We were created to do good works, by which in this brief life we might obtain eternal blessedness, to which all are called by the grace of God. Thus, this present life of ours is the time for continuous physical and spiritual works, while in the future life we will be rewarded according to our works.

St. Moses

If the inner man is not instructed in the Law of God, nor nourished and fortified with reading and prayer, then he is defeated from without, and then he labours for whomever defeated him. From this we see works pleasing to them, but not pleasing to God, such as pride, greed, gluttony, every sort of lustful sin, idle talking, laughing, carousing, drunkenness, malice, cunning, lying, envy, laziness, etc. These are the fruits of sowing to the flesh (Gal.6:8), and why flesh and blood cannot inherit the kingdom of God (I Cor. 15:50).

St. Moses

When a soul is instructed in the Law of God and the body submits to the prudence of the soul, then these works are evident: love for God and neighbour, peace with everyone, modesty, abstinence, chastity, forgiveness, etc. These works are the fruits of the Holy Spirit, and are called sowing to the spirit (Gal. 6:8).

St. Moses

A good work is not accomplished easily, but everything comes with labor and patience.

St. Moses

The fruit of a good deed is love and humility, from which is born peace and a clear conscience.

St. Macarius

Your few works, done with all your infirmity, if offered with repentance and self-reproach, will be received by God more favourably than great feats and labors performed with arrogance and a high opinion of oneself.

St. Macarius

It is not good to place our hope in our works. If we have no love or humility, we will receive no benefit from the works, even though we performed them. Humility alone is powerful enough to save us. We should sincerely try to acquire humility and hope in the merits of our Saviour and His mercy.

St. Macarius

AUDACITY

If you interrupt a conversation, it is an act of audacity.

St. Ambrose

GOOD VIRTUES

Will our insignificant virtues really save us? Do you not remember the words of God? *All our righteousness is as a filthy rag.* (Isaiah, 64:6) Seek rather, the mercy of our Master, not payment for your labors; and you will be saved sooner than thoughtless laborers.

St. Anatoly

Struggle according to your own strength, not considering what you deserve, and do not count your good works. Instead, take notice and enumerate your sins and infirmities, and the Lord will never leave you.

St. Anatoly

Every person who desires to attain the kingdom of Christ must not look back and remember his lofty good deeds, especially his lofty thoughts. One must look at the struggles and glory of the saints, and how God stood by them! Instead, look at your own infirmities and sins, the departure of the soul, and the terrible torments in the next life – and you will not sin.

St. Anatoly

Faith compels us to believe, hope – to trust, love – to love God, and these three virtues are equally needed by us for our salvation. Without these virtues, no one will be granted the joy of seeing God, and no one can be saved.

St. Leo

Wisdom consists not only of sharpness of mind, foresight and prudence, but also skill and the knowledge of how to act.

St. Ambrose

FRIENDSHIP

Every friendship that is not based on true love and humility, but is passionate, is unstable and will fall apart.

St. Macarius

THE SPIRITUAL LIFE

There are times that are sorrowful, wearisome, and dark, and they are unavoidable. In the sensual war, there are afflictions and illness to be endured, but we can receive far worse wounds from the demons in spiritual warfare. As long as we rely on our own abilities and understanding, we will be defeated, until we humble ourselves and acknowledge our infirmity.

St. Macarius

Our life can be likened to a deep ditch, which in times of rain fills up so much that it cannot be crossed, and at other times it dries up and no water flows in it. The Holy Fathers lauded the life that flows like a small stream which flows continually, never running dry. This small stream is good because it is always easy to cross and because it is pleasing and healthy, its water being good for drinking since it flows peacefully and is never murky.

St. Ambrose

In time of battle, resist with humility, as the Fathers have shown us in their writings. But if you should fall into sin, get up again, and realize that you were tempted because of your pride. Flee to self-reproach and humility, but never flee from your cell. Until a monk is broken through various temptations and sorrows, he cannot know his own infirmities and be humbled.

St. Macarius

Spiritual life does not consist of enjoying peace and consolation, but the spiritual cross, that is, gladly enduring the taking away of consolations.

St. Macarius

He who is more inclined to the interior life should take even greater care to leave everyone and everything to the judgement of God and should especially beware of duplicity, lest the words of St. James, the brother of the Lord, be fulfilled in us: *A double-minded man is unstable in all his ways.* (James 1:8)

St. Ambrose

Do not quench the spirit, but rather warm it with patient prayer and with the reading of the Holy Scriptures and writings of the Holy Fathers, cleansing the heart of the passions.

St. Barsanuphius

It is better to agree to endure a thousand deaths than to depart from the divine commandments of the Holy Gospel and the wondrous monastic precepts.

St. Barsanuphius

In the spiritual life, this always happens: either consolation comes before sorrows, or sorrows come just before consolation. These changes give birth to hope and humility. Sorrows are manifested in different ways: physical and spiritual, but it is yet too early for you to know about this. Just accept whatever God sends to you with gratitude and equanimity; do not be exalted from feelings of consolation, and do not despair in times of sorrow.

St. Macarius

In every situation, always try to be pleasant, that is, maintain a peaceful and humble spirit. Do not judge, or grieve anyone, striving so that your words, according to the commandments of the apostles, will be mixed with spiritual salt.

St. Ambrose.

Be courageous in your struggle, and do not falter, even though hell itself rises up against you, and the whole world seethes with malice and ill will against you; *The Lord is near to all who call upon Him in truth.* (Ps. 144:18)

St. Barsanuphius

Whenever you have the intention of doing something that is good, expect temptations from the opposing forces who hate this. You already understand this sufficiently, and you know what is needed to repulse them and defeat them: the acknowledgement of your own infirmities, self-reproach, humility, and seeking God's help.

St. Macarius

There is physical blindness and deafness. It is difficult to endure them, but spiritual deafness and blindness are much worse. May the Lord deliver us from these!

St. Barsanuphius

A SPIRITUAL FATHER

If someone, relying on his own understanding, thinks that he has no need of a guide, he very quickly will stray from the correct path. Therefore, we must implore the

Lord God with tears that He grant to us a wise instructor; owing to the seriousness of our malady, a physician who is experienced and skillful is needed. Therefore, the one who is ill must seek not so much a large and peaceful hospital, as he should a skillful physician.

St. Anthony

Fathers are not fathers only when they pat their children on the head and pamper them, but they are also called fathers when they instruct and punish the child.

St. Anthony

Like medical physicians, spiritual physicians do not all act in the same way. Some will allow the patient to eat and drink everything, while others will order them to keep to a strict diet. It is similar with spiritual fathers; there are those who absolve and forgive everything, while there are others who will interrogate you and who will impose a penance on you for everything; but the aim of them all is the same: to heal you.

St. Anthony

A spiritual father, like a sign-post, merely indicates the way, but you yourself must follow the path. If the spiritual father points the way, but his disciple does not move, and will not go anywhere, then he will simply rot at that sign-post.

St. Nikon

Our Lord Jesus Christ, while praying in the garden of Gethsemane, was to a certain degree an image of every spiritual father in relation to his spiritual children, for he takes their sins upon himself. What a great work, and what only he must endure!

St. Nikon

Why is it necessary to have a spiritual father? In order that you may make your journey and not get lost and may be able to reach the heavenly kingdom. For this, it is necessary, chiefly, to perform in deed the instructions, advice, and directions of the spiritual father, and to piously conduct one's life. There were examples where some were able to visit their elder often, and others continually sat next to their elder, unceasingly heard his instructions, and even lived with him, and yet they remained without fruit. While others had rare opportunity to visit their elder and were granted brief instruction, but they prospered. So in order not to remain fruitless, it is not essential to visit one's spiritual father often, but rather to fulfill his instructions.

St. Nikon

It is pleasing to God that people be guided by other people. In short, every monk must enter the struggle with self-denial and must force himself, with pain of heart, to the warfare with passions. If he will not struggle in such a way, no kind of elder will help him. One God-pleasing man said, "The elder weeps for him (the disciple) and is praying, but he is playing."

St. Nikon

Complete contentment is the result of absolute obedience and faith in one's spiritual father.

St. Nikon

If a person sincerely seeks salvation with his whole heart, God will lead him to a true instructor. Do not worry, each will find the one who is just right for him.

St. Leo

SPIRITUAL UNDERSTANDING

One must use all possible means to support and calm oneself and one's neighbour. Of all means, the principle one is humble supplication to the Lord and placing one's infirmities, and one's neighbour's, on His Almighty help and deliverance. What is possible for us to correct is, without a doubt, possible for God, by Whom we live and move.

St. Moses

HOLY ORDERS

How can one laugh at a clergyman? So what if he serves poorly? He still has grace. He is ordained. One must not, must not, laugh!

St. Anatoly

THE SOUL

The soul is greater than the body: the body becomes sick, and with that it is finished. But a spiritual sickness extends into eternity. Deliver us, O Lord, from such illness, and grant us healing.

St. Macarius

In your patience possess ye your souls (Luke 21:19). Therefore do not become weak and despair when you have the chance to possess your soul. To possess your soul means to give it the significance and place which it was appointed by God, i.e., royal, like unto God, venerated, holy. To not do this means to destroy your soul. *For what is a man profited, if he shall gain the whole world, and lose his soul?* (Matt. 16:26). Therefore, always have in mind first the spiritual welfare of others, and then what is physically necessary: comforts, tranquility, and perhaps, time for relaxation.

St. Anatoly

The heart is not a splinter, and the human soul—not a cheap thing; it is more valuable than all the world. All the treasures on earth and in the universe are not worth one Christian soul.

St. Anatoly

The human soul conceals much good in its depths. One must only search for it.

St. Leo

Just as our physical bodies have various illnesses, so also with the soul. There is physical blindness and there is spiritual blindness. Besides this, there are others who have a kind of dark water in their eyes, so that even though they look, they do not see anything. Similarly, there is a dark water in spiritual eyes due to which they do not see anything.

St. Anthony

THE GOSPEL

In order to fulfill the commandments of Christ, you must know them. They are expounded in the Gospels. Read the Holy Gospel, penetrate its spirit, make it the rule of your life, your manual in everything you do and for every question in life, act in accordance with the teachings of the Gospels. This is the one light in our life.

St Nikon

What wondrous words are in the Gospel .... Whatever book you might take, even the very best author's, if you read it many times, you will get sick of it. But the Gospel—the more you read it, the more you receive comfort and every good feeling.

St. Nikon

I advise you to read the Gospel more often and longer, especially the Gospel of John. Read it so that only your ears hear it: whether you understand it or not, read. The grace-filled words of the Gospel will mightily drive away boredom and despondency and bring comfort; only read it more often and longer.

St. Ambrose

PENANCE

For not fulfilling and neglecting your monastic rule, place this penance on yourself: do not judge anyone, forgive everyone, and in your soul consider yourself worse than everyone in the world. In this way, all your omissions can be forgiven, and a multitude of sins remitted. This is an easy penance which will benefit everyone.

St. Joseph

HERESY

Do not fear sorrows, but fear the stubbornness of heretics who try to separate a man from Christ, which is why Christ commanded us to consider them as pagans and pharisees.

St. Anatoly

THE PATH OF LIFE

We must live on the earth like a wheel that is rolling—only one part touches the earth, while the rest is always moving upwards. But we, being bound to the earth, cannot even stand up.

St. Ambrose

Life is blessedness, and not simply because we believe in blessed eternity, but here on earth life can be blessed if we live with Christ, fulfilling His holy commandments. If a man is not tied to earthly goods, but will in all things rely on the will of God, will live for Christ and in Christ, then life here on earth will become blessed.

St. Barsanuphius

On the path of life, one unfailingly meets sorrows and temptations. One must be ready for them. Our human weakness does not want them and often forgets that they are inevitable, and wants only earthly happiness.

St. Nikon

They who expect and seek comforts and a peaceful life are mistaken: sorrows, deprivations, and difficulties are essential for salvation. If life is so changeable and transient, why become attached to it?

St. Nikon

We live in a vale of tears. Therefore we must pass the time sometimes weeping, sometimes leaping. Let us comfort ourselves with the thought that this vale of tears is temporary. Everything will quickly pass by, will flash by like a shadow, like an echo, and eternity will begin, permanent, unchanging, unending, and hopefully for us, blessed and radiant! Let us hope that the Lord, according to His limitless mercy, will not deprive us of His grace.

St. Ambrose

The external world, with its beauty, acts favourably on a man, and a soul capable of enjoying the beauty of the world becomes exalted. But a man who has achieved perfection sees in his soul such beauty before which the visible world is worthless. Concerning the soul of a man who loves God, the Lord said, *And we will come and make Our abode with him* (John 14:23). It is inscrutable how the Lord Himself dwells in a little heart, but where the Lord is, there is paradise and the Kingdom of God. *The kingdom of God is within you* (Luke 17:21).

St. Barsanuphius

All of life passes in vanity. The mind moves amid vain thoughts and temptations. Gradually, it gets used to remembering God, so that amid vanities and troubles, when not thinking, it will suddenly think, and when not remembering, will suddenly remember Him, just as long as it keeps going without stopping. As long as it is striving forward—do not fear, your little ship is whole, and under the shadow of the Cross it will finish sailing across the sea of life. It is whole and you need not fear what storms may arise. In normal sailing, you cannot avoid inclement weather, and even more so in the path of life. But the misfortunes and storms of life are not frightening for those travelling under the protection of the saving prayer: Lord Jesus Christ, Son of God, have mercy on me, a sinner. They are not frightening, only do not fall into despondency, for despondency gives birth to despair, and despair is already a mortal sin.

St. Barsanuphius

If you happen to sin—believe in the mercy of God; offer up repentance and keep going without being disturbed.

St. Barsanuphius

All of life is a wonderful mystery known only to God. In life, there is not just an accidental chain of events—everything is providential. We do not understand the meaning of this or that event; before us is a multitude of boxes, but no keys. There were once such people who could open them . . .

St. Barsanuphius

To live–do not grieve, do not judge anyone, do not vex anyone, and to everyone my regards.

St. Ambrose

One can live in the world, only not in the limelight, but quietly.

St. Ambrose

CARES

It is not bad that you are learning to manage the household. You consist of not only a soul, but also a body, and the body is needed for the salvation of the soul. One should care for it also.

St. Macarius

ENVY

Envy comes from pride, as well as not fulfilling what is necessary. Cain was careless in offering the required sacrifice to God. But when God rejected his sacrifice because of his carelessness and accepted the fervent sacrifice of Abel, then, because of envy, he decided to kill the righteous Abel. It is best to try to exterminate envy at the very start with humble prayer, humble confession, and prudent silence.

St. Ambrose

In the beginning, envy is revealed through inappropriate zeal and rivalry, and later by fervour with spite and the blaming of the one who is envied.

St. Ambrose

What torments an envious person? The good fortune or preference of a neighbour; although he himself has the same fortune and at times is also given preference, it is annoying to him that his neighbour has these. But where there is love and humility, all the nuances of envy are burned up.

St. Macarius

THE COMMANDMENTS OF GOD

Most of our sins happen because we forget the commandments of God.

St. Nikon

It is indispensable for us to force ourselves to keep the commandments of God. And God's help is always with us.

St. Nikon

When fulfilling the commandments of God we must have humility, and if the power of the commandments weakens in us, then humility will intercede for us. But when we do good works and want to be assured that we are being saved, and see salvation in the palm of our hand, then we are very much mistaken. We should do good works without noticing them, and credit our correction to God and His help, and truly humble ourselves, not falsely.

St. Macarius

We must strive so that all our life, as a whole, and not certain hours and days, is based on the Law of God. We must arrange all of our activities so that they are in agreement with the will of God. Only under these conditions will our heart be pure, and *only the pure in heart will see God* (Matt. 5:8).

St. Nikon

Let us maintain our faith in Christ and according to our strength, fulfill His holy commandments. Only do not rely on your own powers, but on help from the Lord: "Lord help me!"—and He will help.

St. Barsanuphius

The will of God is seen in His commandments, which we must strive to fulfill in our relations with our neighbours, but in cases of breaking and not fulfilling them, we must offer repentance. Our will is corrupted and continuously needs to be forced to fulfill the will of God, and we must implore His help.

St. Macarius

It is necessary for a man to personally begin a new life according to the understanding of the Holy Gospel and the Holy Church of Christ—both in one's outward actions and in one's soul.

St. Nikon

The law of his God is in his heart, and his steps shall not be tripped (Ps. 36:31). When a man places the Law of God and the holy commandments of God in his heart, so to speak, and loves them, then he comes to hate sin; he becomes inflamed with a desire for life in the Lord, and he restrains himself from every sin.

St. Nikon

One must once and for always humbly submit to the requirements of the Church, as if they were not difficult. And they are definitely not difficult!

St. Barsanuphius

He who recognizes himself as an unworthy sinner weeps for his sins. And he who realizes his unworthiness and weeps for his sins cannot give in to anger. He will be meek, according to the example of the Savior Who said, *Learn of Me; for I am meek and lowly in heart* (Matt. 11:29).

St. Nikon

Too much stress is harmful. You can mistakenly lose your strength and become weak. You must surround yourself with the iron ring of the commandments. You must perform every action only after you have verified whether it is in accordance with the commandments, with Holy Scripture. And you should pronounce your words only after you have prayed and considered them.

St. Nikon

Sin concealed by a mask of good sneaks up and harms the souls of those who do not verify themselves with the Gospel. Evangelical good requires self-sacrifice, "the cutting off of one's will and understanding."

St. Nikon

In order to not lose the grace of God, strive more to acquire the remembrance of God. One must fulfill the word of God, i.e., the commandments, as the Lord Himself said: *He that hath My commandments, and keepeth them, he it is that loveth Me* (John 14:21). In such a way there is achieved sincere service to God, with all one's heart.

St. Nektary

You should love your neighbour, but sincerely, not with calculation. Love—it is most beautiful, most holy. It is so beautiful! But people have distorted it. It must be like that of Christ, when He suffered for us.

St. Nektary

A serpent, when it wants to change its old skin for a new one, passes through a very tight and narrow opening, and in this way, it is easy for it to shed its old skin. So also, when a man wants to shed the old man, he must travel the narrow path of fulfilling the commandments of the Gospel.

St. Ambrose

Our life is not arranged arbitrarily, but by Divine Providence. Peace is acquired by cutting off your will. It is impossible to find complete satisfaction. The Lord does not demand the impossible from us, and the fulfillment of the commandments of God is possible everywhere and always. Seeing a person forcing himself to piety in a certain place and situation, according to his strength, and his readiness, the Lord fulfills his desire for good.

St. Nikon

EVIL

With the mask of good remaining in fallen nature, the enemy strives to draw everyone away from Christ, cunningly showing that fallen good is the only good, which is the way it seems to someone who does not know the teachings of Christ. Regardless of all the seductions of the enemy, whoever would adhere to the Gospel teachings must unavoidably experience a struggle within himself. Fallen nature loves itself and loves this world, while the Gospel requires self-sacrifice and love of God. Therefore the two can never be reconciled.

St. Nikon

GOSSIP

If you say something evil about your brother or sister, even if it is true, your soul suffers an unhealable wound. You can reveal the sins of another only when the sole intention in your heart is the benefit of the soul of the sinner.

St. Nikon

ART

Poets and artists who are satisfied only by the delights experienced through art, are like people who arrive at the doors of the Royal Palace, but do not go into the bridal feast, although they are invited to do so.

St. Barsanuphius

TEMPTATIONS

Everyone who even thinks about entering the right path is liable to endure a multitude of all possible temptations. Blessed and most blessed are those who have entered the right path.

St. Barsanuphius

At the beginning of the call to the spiritual life, the Lord visits a person with His grace and various consolations, but afterwards He withdraws them and casts him into the fire of diverse temptations and sorrows, so that our self-loving and glory-loving disposition would be completely reduced to ashes by the fire of temptation, and would not trust in itself and its works but in the mercy and love of God. Humility is a great blessing!

St. Macarius

Everyone needs the fire of temptations in order to be tried and instructed in patience. One must look at things with the point of view that Divine Providence is caring for our salvation: one person requires more, another requires less trials for patience and instruction, and for another, the time has not yet come.

St. Macarius

Do not despair when you experience severe trials: these are necessary for instruction in the spiritual life. Strive to find blame in yourself, but do not blame any of your neighbours.

St. Macarius

Let us humble ourselves and implore the help of God. He can help one who is tempted, for He Himself was tempted.

St. Anatoly

Do not grieve that it has become difficult to live, do not despair, do not be troubled! It is impossible for a young person to cross the stormy sea of the passions without disturbances and the hourly fear of threatening destruction. But this is all temporary: the storm will subside, the glorious sun will begin to shine, and we will reach the cozy, quiet, and always green island. You must be patient!

St. Anatoly

You must not grow faint-hearted. Surely you cannot live without temptations: *Who is the man that shall live and not see death?* (Ps. 88:49), i.e., temptations? Temptation is necessary because it brings about patience, and patience—proficiency. If we were not tried, we would remain ignorant and stupid. In times of trouble, let us accuse ourselves and not others.

St. Anatoly

The freedom of rational faculties has always been tested and until now, is tested until they are confirmed in goodness. This is because goodness is not confirmed without trial. Every Christian is tested by something: one by poverty, another by illness, a third by various bad thoughts, a fourth by some calamity or humiliation, while another by various doubts. And through this, firmness of faith, hope, and love of God are tested.

St. Ambrose

Peace is promised to us in the future life, but here on earth—labour and temptation. *Blessed is the man that endureth temptation* (James 1:12).

St. Moses

Many storms and hurricanes disturb the atmosphere and cause various kinds of destruction, but for all this, King David elicits the praise of God. And the actions of evil spirits, like the storms, disturb the hearts and souls of people on earth. What is there for us, who are infirm, to do? One of the nearest and surest means of help is raising our hands to the Lord God, like Moses in the desert, where the enemy forces of Amalik attacked him. Through the All-Highest God we will surmount the wall of temptations. God is with us. And we must not be overly afraid.

St. Moses

CONFESSION

When approaching the Mystery of Confession, one must present himself with fear, humility, and hope. With fear as before God, Who is angry with the sinner. With humility—through recognition of one's sinfulness. With hope—for we approach the Child-loving Father, Who has sent His Son for our redemption, Who has taken our sins, nailed them to the Cross, and washed them away with His most pure Blood.

St. Macarius

To fear shame during confession is also from pride; they who reproach themselves before God in the presence of a witness receive peace and forgiveness.

St. Macarius

The holy fathers do not recommend explaining sins of sensuality in detail so that the memory of the details do not defile the senses, but to simply confess the kind of sin. The other sins, which bring shame to our self-love, must be confessed in detail, with self-accusation.

St. Macarius

Sinful habits and passions do not give way to healing without confession. Without confession, every healing will be incomplete and insufficient, but with confession, the sins will be uprooted in due order. It is always necessary to pay special attention to confession, to always prepare for it carefully, and sincerely confess all of your sins.

St. Nikon

You need not fear your spiritual father, and you must not be ashamed before him. The spiritual father knows everything, he knows all sins, since he has not just one soul to care for, but he confesses hundreds, and you will not surprise him with any kind of sin, no matter how great or burdensome it may be.

St. Nikon

If a person's conscience is not lost, it will give him no peace until everything is related in detail at confession. You should not relate superfluous details, which do not explain the essence of the matter, but merely vividly portray it. Such a vivid picture of the sin, like a pleasant remembrance of the sin, the fathers advise not to allow ourselves, especially in matters of fornication, so that the heart, which still loves sin, does not linger and enjoy the sin.

St. Nikon

Many people seek, as if essential, a spiritual father who leads an exalted life, and they become despondent when they do not find such a one, and therefore they rarely, almost reluctantly, come to confession. This is a great mistake. You need to believe in the very Mystery of Confession, in its power, not in the person who performs the Mystery. It is essential only that the spiritual father be Orthodox and authorized by the Church. You need not argue that the personal qualities of the spiritual father are important, but you should believe and know that the Lord, active in every Mystery through His Grace, acts according to His omnipotence, regardless of these qualities.

St. Nikon

It is a precious thing to have a pious spiritual father with whom you can seek advice and clarify this or that question in the spiritual life and simply talk, in order to warm your cold heart with spiritual conversation and receive spiritual strength amid the sorrows that surround us.

St. Nikon

Whoever confesses his sins with simplicity of heart, with feelings of compunction and humility and the desire to correct himself, will receive forgiveness of sins and peace of conscience through the power of the grace of God acting in the Mystery.

St. Nikon

If you are attracted to something through weakness, do not become faint-hearted and confused, but strive to correct this through self-reproach and confession, first to

God the Knower of hearts, and later to your spiritual father. Let these passionate attractions teach you, through restraint, carefulness, guarding yourself, and through the fear of God. Entrust yourself to the will of God, and with patience wait for your fate to be resolved.

St. Ambrose

CORRECTION

We have come in order to learn the spiritual life: what is so surprising if we sin? Let us correct ourselves! and God Himself will correct us!

St. Anatoly

Whoever is attentive to himself and sorry for his shallow life and seeks help from God, will, even against his own will, go the way of the publican praised in the Gospel.

St. Anatoly

Condemn yourself and try to correct yourself. But we cannot correct ourselves if we do not begin with self-reproach (and not reproaching others) and with forcing ourselves to be obedient to our elders.

St. Anatoly

Whoever has a wicked heart need not despair, for with the help of God, a person can correct his heart. He must only watch over himself carefully and not pass up any opportunity to help his neighbour, reveal his thoughts to his elder often, and give alms as much as possible. This, of course, cannot all be done at once, but the Lord is Long-suffering.

St. Ambrose

In order for a man to correct himself, he does not need to suddenly throw himself into the task, but he should approach it as they who pull a barge: pull, pull, pull, let go! – Not all at once, but little by little. You know the cleat on a ship? It is a kind of pole to which are tied all the ropes of the ship. If they pull on it suddenly, everything will be destroyed from the sudden shock.

St. Ambrose

TRIALS

No matter what sorrows they may be, they are like the smallest sparks, i.e., if you spit—you will extinguish them. But if you will fan the smallest spark, a flame will arise which will entirely destroy the good condition of the person. This fanning is from many thoughts; for example: "My heart is under a heavy cross; monastic life is truly bitter; my whole heart is torn to pieces."

St. Anthony

The weather is severe, rain, wind and cold, so that even with a fur coat you have to run for more fuel for the fire. But fresh air and clear weather are also not always beneficial: worms and other insects appear in the plants, damaging the good fruit. This happens in our spiritual formation as well. If the presence of grace, peace, quiet, and freedom from the attacks of the passions is prolonged and remains with us continuously, it is dangerous because we can develop high-mindedness and be deprived of protection. We will then not be skilled in battling the passions and will depart from the path of sorrow. Therefore, God tries us with unpleasant things, so that we can see our infirmities, for our patience and humility.

St. Macarius

On earth, everything is temporary, brief and transitory. Soon everything will pass by, that which is pleasant and delightful, just as what is lamentable and sorrowful. If we have chosen for ourselves the path of piety, then we must remember and not forget the words of the Apostle: *All that will live godly in Christ shall suffer persecution* (II Tim., 3:12).

St. Ambrose

Strive to live this way—by necessity or chance, some people are walking through the forest. They come across a gnarled tree and they either bend down to get under it, or go around it, but somehow a pesky branch whips against the back of their head. But they pay it little attention.

St. Ambrose

THE MONASTIC CELL

You are doing well when you sit at home. St. Arsenius the Great taught: "Sit in your cell and it will teach you everything (good)." Sit with God and Christ Himself will come to you. Just maintain the prayer: "Lord Jesus Christ, Son of God, have mercy on me a sinner."

St. Anatoly

After the all-night vigil, they come to you in your cell; then stand, light a candle and say: "Well, Sister Barbara, you read the evening prayers" —and each in turn. This way you will wean them from coming to your cell.

St. Ambrose

THE CELL RULE

Always read the morning and evening prayers from the prayer book, investigating with attention the meaning of each word and delving deeply into it. Use the prayer rope in church, but when you are home... . Read daily a chapter from the Gospels and the Epistles and Acts of the Apostles. If you want to converse more intimately with the Lord, read a kathisma or the Akathist to Our Sweetest Lord Jesus or the Mother of God.

St. Anatoly

If there is time during your cell rule, use it accordingly in the study of books and in writing. When other activities do not allow time for this, then peacefully forbear the studies for the sake of obedience. Labor according to your strength, but not too much, so that you do not become despondent due to excess. Take care in your conversation and be on your guard with the brethren. Whatever food you receive, with the blessing of the elder, partake of it giving glory to God. Endure unpleasantness and insufficiencies for the sake of God.

St. Moses

When you fulfill your prayers and your rule, thank God, but when you do not fulfill it, accuse yourself.

St. Anatoly

The reading of the prayer rule: it should be read with humility and the fear of God, not so that people praise you, but so that you read with attention, and if you are distracted and accept praise, immediately reproach yourself.

St. Macarius

It is better not to neglect a small prayer rule than to take on a big one.

St. Macarius

The Lord does not demand a prayer rule, especially from the sick and the weak—but humility is always necessary. It fulfills what is lacking in the prayer rule. What is humility? To consider yourself worse than everyone else, to judge no one, to not complain, etc.

St. Macarius

Do not take on any kind of vows and prayer rules without the approval of your spiritual father, with whose advice one prostration will bring more benefit than a thousand performed from self-will. Believe this without a doubt.

St. Anthony

When someone is performing his cell rule and he feels a special urging of the spirit for the Jesus Prayer or for studying the Holy Scriptures, then he can leave the cell rule for a while and occupy himself with one or the other activity. This is what experienced fathers teach us.

St. Ambrose

When there is not enough time, it is better to read only part of the prayer rule, but with attention. Fearful are the words spoken in the Holy Scriptures: *Cursed is the man that doeth the works of the Lord carelessly* (Jeremiah 48:10).

St. Nikon

Not everyone is able to stand at prayer often during the course of the day. But everyone can force himself to pray, even if just mentally, if in the presence of others. It is possible to begin and end every work and activity by raising the mind to God. A cold-hearted attitude toward the work of prayer is not helpful: "I've said my prayers, I've read what I was told to do, and now I am free. I've done my duty." Such prayer does not produce good fruit.

St. Nikon

SLANDER

A weak person prays that no one slanders him, a courageous person prays that God will help him not to slander others, neither in word nor thought.

St. Ambrose

WITCHCRAFT

The enemy has no power to do anything against those who live righteously and do the will of the Lord. When, with a whole legion, Satan himself did not dare enter into a herd of swine, but asked permission for this from our Lord Jesus Christ, Who then cast this legion from the man, what harm then can he do to a man when the Lord allows it as punishment, for testing his faith?

St. Macarius

THE CROSS

It has been so arranged by the Lord God, that in His care for the salvation of our soul, each person in this life has a cross which he must humbly carry to our Heav-

enly Father from his childhood, calling to Him from the depth of his soul: "Our Father! May Thy Holy Will be done in all things, only do not deprive me of Thy Heavenly Kingdom."

St. Anthony

To bear the cross does not mean only visible, external sorrows, but also internal spiritual ones. One must endure darkness, faintheartedness and similar things as well. For God sends this for the destruction of our pride and acquiring of humility.

St. Macarius

We seek and desire sweet, spiritual enjoyment; I do not argue, it is pleasant—but it is lower than the cross. It is granted to us through the cross and without the cross it cannot last. It comes to us and leaves us according to the degree that we travel the way of the cross and humility.

St. Macarius

Everyone bears his cross, and you bear your cross, even though it is only the size of a finger; you still bear it. The bearing of a cross is absolutely necessary for every Christian for his salvation, and not only for monks. Yes, everyone bears a cross, and has borne a cross; even the Incarnate God bore a cross, and His Cross was the heaviest, as if combining in itself all the crosses of mankind. And take note: God is carrying the cross and a man (Simon the Cyrenian) helps Him. He takes the cross from Him and carries it himself. This means that by bearing our crosses we help the Lord to carry the cross, i.e., we are preparing to be His servants in heaven in the choir of bodiless Spirits.... What a high calling!

St. Barsanuphius

THE SIGN OF THE CROSS

We faithful have a great weapon—this is the power of the Life-giving Cross. Think how terrifying it becomes for unbelievers; they are completely helpless. It is as if a person set out completely unarmed into the thick forest at night. Yes, the first beast he came across would tear him up, and he would have nothing to defend himself with. But we will not be afraid of the demons! The power of the sign of the Cross and the name of Jesus is terrifying to the enemies of Christ, and saves us from the evil nets of the demons.

St. Barsanuphius

One must make the sign of the cross on oneself, either with the name of the Holy Trinity, saying "In the name of the Father, and of the Son, and of the Holy Spirit," or with the name of One of the Trinity, Who became incarnate for our sake and was voluntarily crucified, saying, "Lord Jesus Christ, Son of God, have mercy on me, a sinner."

St. Ambrose

SMOKING

You can't stop smoking tobacco? What is impossible for man is possible with God's help. Just firmly decide to quit, realizing how harmful it is for the soul and the body, since tobacco weakens the soul, and increases and strengthens the passions, darkens the mind, and destroys physical health with a slow death.

St. Ambrose

LAZINESS

Laziness is not a small vice and it is numbered among the mortal sins, and therefore we must force ourselves to fulfill our duties and ask God for help and not rely on our own strength. Seeing our good intentions, He will give strength and power and will help us overcome the paralyzing laziness; but without our effort and good intention, God does not help. During time of infirmity and weakness, let these take the place of our idleness: pain of heart, remorse, and humility.

St. Macarius

Laziness often attacks those who labor in piety, and frequently it overcomes a person when he is negligent. To drive away this passion, the holy fathers advise us to hold on to the memory of death, eternal torments, and the blessedness of the righteous, being guided in this with humility, which, by drawing down upon us the mercy of God, will completely free us from the captivity of laziness.

St. Macarius

Against laziness–courage and the fear of God.

St. Macarius

In the course of prayer, there sometimes occur dreams, laziness, melancholy, and coldness towards everything, lasting for a few days and even a week. It probably happened that before this we were secretly plundered by the enemy through vainglory, pride, judging others, anger, or something else. The spiritual enemy does violence to our nature so that we pass our days in idleness and laziness, rather than preparing for eternity. But if we are overcome due to our infirmity, let us not be despondent because of this, but instead let us humble ourselves and struggle with the help of God. The power of God is made perfect in infirmity.

St. Anatoly

Strive to struggle against laziness and drive it away and force yourself to labor in prayer. Remember that you must unfailingly force yourself in order to receive salvation.

St. Joseph

MEDICAL TREATMENT

The Lord created doctors and medicine. You must not refuse treatment.

St. Nikon

A monk should not undergo serious medical treatment, but be treated only for a while.

St. Ambrose

You must treat incurable diseases with faith, fleeing to God and His saints; but when someone does not receive healing, then it is evident that he must carry this cross, sent for the salvation of his soul.

St. Macarius

CRAFTINESS

He who desires to acquire a good conscience and honesty must not permit himself even the slightest false or crafty word, neither in important matters, nor the unimportant.

St. Nikon

LOVE OF GOD

The feeling of love of the Lord corresponds to how much we fulfill His commandments.

St. Nikon

Love of God is expressed most of all by keeping the commandments of God.

St. Nikon

When giving all of yourself to God, you must not worry about rags and attach your heart to them.

St. Anthony

You cannot serve God and mammon (Matt. 6:24); you cannot serve God and sin. According to the Gospel, *man must love the Lord with all his soul, with all his strength, all his heart, and all his mind* (Matt. 22:37; Mark 12:30; Luke 10:27), giving sin not one sense, not one of your talents, either spiritual or physical.

St. Nikon

If one relies on the will of God—everything good, and even what is unpleasant, everything leads to the salvation of our soul, and in this is revealed great wisdom and profundity. For those that love God all things lead to good.

St. Nikon

Scriptures say that *we must, through much tribulation, enter into the Kingdom of God* (Acts 14:22). See what kind of love we have for the Heavenly Bridegroom! We do not just love and desire Him in word, but in deed, and we weep.

St. Anatoly

LOVE OF NEIGHBOR

The Holy Apostle said, *Children, love one another* (I John 4:7), humble yourselves, humble yourselves. Because if you love someone (and you must love everyone because every person is an image of God, and it, i.e., the image of God, is in even a defiled person, he can be cleansed and again be pure), then you humble yourself before him. Where there is love, there is also humility; but where there is malice—there is pride. I ask and desire that there be love among you.

St. Nikon

You must love every man, seeing in him the image of God, disregarding his vices. You must not dismiss people with coldness.

St. Nikon

He who desires to acquire love must first reject every angry and malicious thought, not to mention action and word, and must forgive all offenses, just and unjust.

St. Nikon

From kindness, people see things entirely different.

St. Ambrose

Love covers everything. And if someone does good to his neighbor through the inclination of the heart, and not out of duty, then the devil cannot interfere; but when it is done out of a sense of duty, then he tries to interfere with one or the other.

St. Ambrose

To one who labors God sends mercy, but to one who loves, consolation.

St. Ambrose

If you will receive people for the sake of God, then be assured that all will be well with you.

St. Ambrose

Love, of course, is above everything. If you find that you have no love, but desire to have it, then perform works of love, although at first without love. The Lord will see your desire and your striving and will put love in your heart. But mainly, when you notice that you have sinned against love, immediately confess it to your elder. This can happen sometimes from a foolish heart, and sometimes from the enemy. You yourself cannot discern this, but when you confess, the enemy will go away.

St. Ambrose

There is no higher virtue than love, and there is no vice or passion worse than hatred, which, for someone who is not attentive to himself, seems of little importance, but in spiritual significance is likened to murder (I John 3:15). Kindness and condescension to your neighbors, and forgiveness of their shortcomings, is the shortest path to salvation.

St. Ambrose

Above all, strive to love your neighbor, for in his love consists love for God.

St. Macarius

Love for God is proven by love and mercy for your neighbor, and mercy, charity, condescension for your neighbor, and forgiveness of his shortcomings are acquired through humility and self-reproach, when in all grievous and unpleasant situations we place the blame on ourself and not on others, realizing that we did not act as we should have and for this reason the unpleasantness and grief occurred; and if we will reason in such a way, we will grieve much less and will not give in to anger, which does not work the righteousness of God.

St. Ambrose

They do not love you—you love them. The fact that they do not love you does not depend on you; but your loving them is within your power and is your duty, for the Lord commanded: do not love just those who love you, but also your enemies (Matt. 5:44). But when there is no love in us, so much more must we humble ourselves, drive away pride, and pray about this to the Lord.

St. Macarius

CURIOSITY

Do not investigate the affairs of others—you will lose peace!

St. Anatoly

FAINTHEARTEDNESS

Every prudent person does not weep in advance, but he waits for whatever the Lord will send him. And what the Lord sends—whether good or bad—he accepts with joy and strives to endure according to his strength. But if he cannot endure—he repents for his faintheartedness. But we become fainthearted beforehand; while still not seeing any misfortune or sorrow, we grieve before the sorrow ever comes. Christian, live in a Christian manner.

St. Anatoly

Faintheartedness often seizes us; this is allowed and happens not only because of very many sins, but even more because of haughtiness.

St. Leo

Again you fall in spirit from every wave of sorrows that are so unavoidable in the world. And where will you flee from them? To Kiev, or beyond Kiev? There is an abundance of them everywhere. But honor and eternal glory are given not to those who speedily flee from them (sorrows), but to those who meet them fearlessly.

St. Anatoly

Enough of childish faintheartedness: a serious matter is at hand–concerning your soul, concerning the eternal Kingdom, which your enemy, the devil, has lost. All the

Heavenly Powers watch how you struggle with the prince of this world, and they implore the Almighty to help you. Yes, He will help, only do not despair! The Lord is near!

St. Anatoly

MODERATION

Moderation in all things is good. There is a spiritual age (of a person) just as there is an outward age. Just as nine-year-olds cannot grasp what is proper for twenty-year-olds, so also in the spiritual life: with zeal that is foolish and beyond your strength, you can spiritually hurt yourself. But if the Lord spares someone from this, at the very least, he will take on the labor and grief in vain. Go slowly—and you'll go farther, as the experienced say. It is harmful not to take care of what is necessary, but it is dangerous to strive for what is beyond your limit. Above all, hold on to these three: fear of God, humility, and constant repentance.

St. Ambrose

MERCY

To be concerned for the good upbringing of children and the care of the elderly and infirm—these are works of mercy, commanded of us Christians by the Lord—for which He promises a reward to all those who fulfill His commandments: *Blessed are the merciful, for they shall obtain mercy* (Matt. 5:7). Therefore, I hope that you will not grow weary of these works of mercy, but pray to the Lord for understanding, to know where, how, and what to say, or how to act, and for help in performing the good work, and then act, according to your strength and ability.

St. Joseph

It is good to conceal the shortcomings of your neighbors when you can and when it brings no harm; but when the shortcomings begin to reveal themselves, it is better to be truthful and trust in the will of God.

St. Joseph

We must show all manner of compassion towards our neighbors, all manner of leniency, and from yourself demand all truth, all righteousness.

St. Ambrose

ALMS

The essence of almsgiving is a heart burning with love for every creature and desiring what is good for it. Almsgiving consists not merely in the giving, but in compassion, when we see a fellow human being suffering in some way, and if we can help him somehow, we do so.

St. Macarius

Spiritual almsgiving is greater than material almsgiving; he who does not share what he himself is using is miserly and unmerciful.

St. Macarius

SPIRITUAL PEACE

God Himself lives in that man who has a peaceful heart. Above all, consider yourself worse than everyone, seek neither love nor honor from anyone, but have them yourself for everyone—thus you will obtain peace. But as soon as you want others to notice the goodness and virtue in you, then say good-bye to spiritual peace!

St. Anatoly

Wherever God is—there is peace. And the opposite is self-evident: where there is envy, enmity, impatience, self-love—there is the devil. Wherever the devil is—there, everything is ruinous, proud and hostile.

St. Anatoly

Endure everything, and you will be at peace and you will bring peace to others! But if you complain about details, you will lose peace and along with it salvation.

St. Anatoly

Whether you live peacefully or not depends on you. If you are patient, you will be peaceful. But if you begin to return evil for evil, peace will depart, and God will leave the mob to serve justice. Where there is peace, there is God. His dwelling is peace.

St. Anatoly

God grant you a peaceful and soul-saving household, in accordance to the example of Christ's teaching, and not the code of civil law—eye for an eye, tooth for a tooth.

St. Moses

Where there is peace, there is God; but where there is enmity, there is the opposite, from which may the Lord deliver us!

St. Macarius

Do not allow the spark of discord and enmity to smolder. The longer you wait, the more the enemy tries to cause confusion among you. Be watchful, so that he does not mock you. Humility destroys all of his schemes.

St. Macarius

By sinning before God we lose peace; but by repentance peace returns, through the mercy of God. We also lose peace when we are grieved and quarrel with people; but when we extinguish this flame with self-reproach, then peace reigns.

St. Macarius

Always have God as your helper and do not trust in your own understanding and strength. Consider yourself to be the least of all, and among yourselves have humility and love in the Lord. Let none of you consider herself superior, but let each consider herself to be the last, and all the other sisters better than herself. Do not notice the faults of others and do not judge, and thus the peace of God will be with you!

St. Macarius

Try to control your senses, especially your eyes. And continue to endure your difficulties with patience and gratitude without complaining, and when, with God's help, you will try to gladly endure the present temptation and will attribute it to your own sins, and when grieved in heart you will pray, according to the Lord's commandment, for those who have sinned against you, then you will clearly feel joy and ineffable consolation in your heart, peace in your thoughts, and love for God and for everyone, not only for those living with you, but for others as well.

St. Leo

The work of our salvation is required everywhere, wherever a person may live: the fulfillment of the Divine commandments and submission to the will of God. Only through this is spiritual peace obtained, and in no other way, as it says in the psalms: *much peace have they that love Thy law, and for them there is no stumbling-block* (Ps. 118:165).

St. Ambrose

THE WORLD

By the word, "world," we understand everything which is subject to the passions, which is far from God. Here we are fine. Glory to God! We live in the desert of the world—we can go to church, we can converse with like-minded people. Glory to God!

St. Nikon

Beware of passionate attachments to the world. Although they deceive you with peace and comfort, they are so fleeting that you do not notice how you are deprived of them, and in their place come sorrow, longing, despondency, and no comfort whatsoever.

St. Leo

Having recognized the truly useless vanity of the world, you should flee from it and seek for yourself a way to fulfill the will of God. But as long as we serve the world, we do not see the darkness of the passions, darkening our thoughts. Being in such a state of blindness, we do not care that by pleasing the world we become violators of the Divine Commandments, and we think that by making a few minor corrections we will become true Christians;

but in this way, we greatly deceive ourselves, not studying the teachings of the Saviour, the Lord Jesus Christ.

St. Macarius

The world—it is such a monster, that if you turn around, it will tear you to pieces.

St. Barsanuphius

When the valve in the heart that is meant for perceiving worldly enjoyments is shut, then another valve opens, for perceiving spiritual enjoyments. But how do you attain this? Before all else, through peace and love for your neighbor. And then through patience. Who will be saved? He who endures to the end (Matt. 10:22). Also—through avoiding sinful pleasures, such as card games, and dances, etc.

St. Barsanuphius

The affairs of the world are so numerous that they could hardly be completed in a hundred years, and so important that they will not allow any kind of delay. To our misfortune, only God-pleasing works can be set aside without fear, some until morning, some until next year, and some even until old age, for which reason it often happens that they remain unfulfilled. I sincerely sympathize but cannot help in any way.

St. Anthony

Can you place your hope in the world? Whom has it not deceived? To whom has it not lied? It promises much, but gives very little. Only those who hope in the Lord, according to the words of the Prophet David, do not sin, i.e., they are not deceived in their hope!

St. Anthony

PRAYER

When you begin to pray, begin to think of your sins and weep for them—this is how you should pray. Afterwards, you sometimes feel peace and joy, and you think that this is from the enemy. But, according to the holy fathers, this joy is from the enemy if it is discordant, not bringing peace and quiet to the soul. And do not be surprised that the Lord grants peace and quiet during prayer, for it does not always happen according to our worthiness, but according to the inscrutable judgements of God. Therefore, when you feel such joy and peace, consider yourself to be entirely unworthy of this gift from God and reproach yourself before the Lord that because of your carelessness you cannot preserve within yourself this gift and soon you will lose it.

St. Joseph

Do not look only for delight from prayer; do not become despondent when you do not feel joy. Sometimes you stand and stand in church, and it seems that you do not have a heart within you, but a piece of wood, rough and coarse. And so what? For the piece of wood, thank You, Lord! It means that that is how it should be. By experiencing sweet delights, a soul can become puffed up, but such a condition of "stony insensibility" humbles it.

St. Barsanuphius

Without Divine help, we are not in a condition to pray on our own; we cannot pray as we should and we do not know how and for what to pray.

St. Nikon

We should pronounce the words of the prayer attentively and penetrate the meaning, but not strive for something too exalted. If we read incorrectly and do not pay attention to what is read, we please the demons.

St. Nikon

During fervent prayer, you want them to see how you are praying. The demons are sowing these vainglorious thoughts. It is good that you do not dwell on them. And in the future you must scorn them.

St. Joseph

Prayer is food for the soul. Do not starve the soul, it is better to let the body go hungry. Do not judge anyone, forgive everyone. Consider yourself worse than everyone in the world and you will be saved. As much as possible, be more quiet.

St. Joseph

Prayer, fasting, and vigilance over ourselves, i.e., carefully watching our thoughts and feelings, make us victors over the enemies of our salvation. The most difficult of these three works is prayer—an everlasting virtue which will become a habit if we practice it. But prayer, until our very death, will require coercion on our part, a constant struggle.

St. Barsanuphius

Prayer to God is always profitable. But precisely how, we do not know. He is the One Righteous Judge, but we can mistake a lie for the truth. Pray and believe.

St. Anatoly

Do not attach your heart to worldly vanity. Especially during prayer, put aside all worldly thoughts. After prayer, whether in church or at home, silence is necessary in order to preserve the prayerful, compunctionate mood of the soul. Sometimes a seemingly simple, even insignificant word can destroy and scare off, like a little bird, the compunction from our soul.

St. Nikon

Do not forget prayer—it is the life of the soul.

St. Nikon

It is necessary to preserve the fruit of prayer. It is spoiled and lost very often due to idle talking right after prayer and from dreaming, which is also idle talking, only with yourself. Silence after prayer is very beneficial: it keeps the prayer in the mind, heart, and even in the mouth, audible to you.

St. Nikon

We must not attribute miracle-working power to our prayer; we must not think that what we ask of the Lord is always fulfilled. This thought comes from pride and leads to deception.

St. Hilarion

At all times, whatever you may be doing: whether you are sitting, or walking, or working, say with the heart, "Lord have mercy."

St. Nektary

Pray that the Lord will rule in your heart. Then it will overflow with great rejoicing and happiness, and no kind of sorrow will have the strength to disturb it.

St. Nektary

The power of prayer is not in many words, but in the sincerity of a prayerful sigh.

St. Nektary

Whoever the Lord visits with a difficult ordeal, sorrow, the bereavement of a dearly beloved one, such a person involuntarily prays with all his heart, all his understanding, all of his mind. Consequently, there is a wellspring of prayer in everyone, but it is revealed either by gradually going deeper and deeper into yourself, according to the teaching of the fathers, or by a sudden Divine drilling into one's soul.

St. Leo

It is good to pray while standing before the crucifixion, recalling the sufferings of the Saviour: the spitting upon, the slapping, the mocking, the beating. The spirit is humbled in this way.

St. Ambrose

Pray for yourself, seeking only the mercy and will of God; whether you are in church or outside of church, walking, sitting or lying down, pray: "Lord have mercy, however You think best, however You will".

St. Ambrose

God does not demand undistracted prayer from beginners. It is acquired with much time and labor, as the writings of the holy fathers say: "God grants prayer to those who pray... ."

St. Hilarion

In the struggle of prayer, it is absolutely necessary to force oneself, and compel oneself to pray.

St. Barsanuphius

When you cannot be in church on a weekday, get up earlier and read some prayers for your consolation.

St. Ambrose

When you do not have much time for prayer, be satisfied with the time that you do have, and God will accept your good desire. Remember that the feeling of the Publican in prayer is pleasing to God, and beware of evaluating your prayer: that is the work of God, not us.

St. Macarius

The work of prayer is such that, having lived in the monastery for a few years, you still do not quickly learn to pray as you should; but now for the time being, pray however you can and are able, only with the thought of the Publican.

St Ambrose

I ask you to pray for those who have offended you, saying: "O Lord, Who lovest mankind, forgive those who hate us and offend us, Thy servants (their names), for they know not what they do, and warm their heart to love us unworthy ones."

St. Anthony

The Lord prayed for those who crucified Him, and the protomartyr St. Stephen prayed for those killing him, that it would not be counted as a sin for them, saying, "For they know not what they do." Do likewise and you will receive mercy and Divine help, and you will be at peace.

St. Ambrose

Pray for those who grieve you, with these words: "Save, O Lord, so and so..., and by her prayers have mercy on me a sinner." Especially pray in this way in time of great confusion. At the same time it is good to make full prostrations, if there is room.

St. Ambrose

You must pray for those who hate and offend you thus: "Save, O Lord, and have mercy on Thy servant, my beloved sister (name), and for the sake of her holy prayers have mercy on me, the wretched sinner."

St. Ambrose

PRAYER IN CHURCH

Concerning prayer in church, know that it is higher than prayers at home, for it is raised by a whole group of people, among which many are most pure prayers, offered to God from humble hearts, which He accepts as fragrant incense. Along with these our prayers are also accepted, even though they are feeble and worthless.

St. Macarius

One should enter the church in a spirit of humility, for prayer is not accepted if we have something against someone or if someone has been grieved by us.

St. Macarius

Prayer in church is important. The best thoughts and feelings come in church, yes, and the enemy attacks more violently in church, but with the sign of the Cross and the Jesus Prayer, you drive him away. It is good to stand in some dark corner in church and to pray to God. "Let us lift up our hearts!" the priest exclaims, but our mind often creeps along the ground, thinking about indecent things. Fight against this.

St. Barsanuphius

During prayer, it is not beneficial to strive for exalted feelings. One should only discern the meaning of the words pronounced, pray attentively, and then, with time, the Lord will grant spiritual insight and heartfelt contrition.

St. Nikon

THE JESUS PRAYER

Pray fervently to the Lord God and warm your cold heart with His sweetest name, for God is our fire. Calling on His name destroys impure dreams and warms the heart to fulfill all of His commandments.

St. Anthony

How can one see Christ? The way to make this possible: the unceasing Prayer of Jesus, which alone is able to bring Christ to dwell in our souls.

St. Barsanuphius

We have one sword—the Prayer of Jesus. It is said, "Strike the unseen enemies with this sword, for there is no more powerful weapon, either in heaven or on earth."

St. Barsanuphius

We who are infirm must unfailingly call out to Jesus, Who came to call not the righteous, but sinners to repentance. And therefore, having neither deeds nor the spiritual powers for ascetic struggles, we must unavoidably call out: Lord Jesus Christ, Son of God, have mercy on us!

St. Anatoly

The path of the Jesus Prayer is the shortest path, the most convenient one. But do not complain, for everyone who travels this path experiences sorrows. Once you've decided to travel this path, go and do not complain if you meet difficulties and sorrows—you must endure.

St. Barsanuphius

In order to always have the memory of God, there is the Jesus Prayer.

St. Barsanuphius

Drive away the enemy and those who bring temptations of evil thoughts with prayer: "Lord Jesus Christ, Son of God, have mercy on me, a sinner." This prayer can be said during all activities.

St. Nektary

With all your might strive to retain the Prayer of Jesus—it is all of our life, all beauty, all consolation; that it is difficult in the beginning is known to everyone, but after that it is priceless, all-joyous, all-loving.

St. Anatoly

Do it according to your strength, do it with humility and self-reproach, and you will get used to and will love the prayer so that they cannot take it from you by force. This is because it is sweet and gives joy. *I remembered God and I was gladdened* (Ps. 76:3).

St. Anatoly

Be prepared to meet sorrows. For the enemy never fails to avenge those who come to enjoy the Prayer of Jesus and he will always "teach" either the elderly or the young, and will play his dirty tricks.

St. Anatoly

Hold on to the Jesus Prayer with all your strength. And when you grow weak, have the remembrance of the presence of God. Do not grieve that your prayer is not unceasing—it is too early for you. But thank God for what there is. Save yourself, and may the Lord save you.

St Anatoly

The work of a monastic must be secret. That is why the holy fathers call the Jesus Prayer the "hidden activity." It should be kept secret even from yourself. Do not sound the trumpet, as it says in the Gospel, not only before others, but even before yourself.

St. Nikon

The acquisition of inner prayer is essential. Without it you cannot enter into the Kingdom of Heaven. Outward mental prayer is insufficient, for it can be present even in a person in whom the passions dwell. Some even say, "What is the sense in praying? What benefit is it?" A great benefit! For the Lord, *Who gives to those who pray* (I Kings 2:9), will give prayer to a person either before his death or even after death... Only, you should not stop praying.

St. Barsanuphius

A wearisome, often cheerless condition, preceding the receiving of the inner Jesus Prayer, does not necessarily happen with everyone. For the king can suddenly make a poor man rich. But the general rule of acquiring the Jesus Prayer is that they attain it with labors and sorrows, among which is a wearisome state of soul.

St. Barsanuphius

One can say the Jesus Prayer while in the company of others, with the mind, quietly pronouncing the words without opening your lips, but mainly one needs humility with the feeling of the Publican.

St. Macarius

One can retain the prayer mentally during sickness, when infirm, when with people and during work. Only sometimes the head aches, but what can you do? After that one comes to like it. A thousand times over comes to like it. Try to hold the thought with Jesus not only in the head, but direct it a little toward the chest. Then, of course, the chest will hurt, but without this it is impossible. Our God is a consuming fire. And where it is impure—there it hurts. Such pain is sent because of our unworthiness. But in time, it will pass.

St. Anatoly

In the beginning the Prayer of Jesus is always difficult and not pure, but later it is pleasant.

St. Anatoly

The prayer has ceased—of course there is a reason for this: either self-opinion, or judging others. The main thing is that we be humble.

St. Anatoly

Let your first task, as soon as you awaken, be the sign of the cross, and your first words—the words of the Jesus Prayer.

St. Barsanuphius

Prayer can cease only because of serious sins. Or if someone does not repent and is not watchful over himself. But if someone repents, he needs this prayer. You only need to keep yourself in depth of humility and worthlessness. But in order for prayer to be firmly established, the very best means is to endure sorrows and scorn.

St. Anatoly

Say the Jesus Prayer more often—it will gladden the heart. Only strive to pluck out the rotten stuff from the heart, i.e., do not be attracted by unchaste thoughts.

St. Anatoly

The Jesus Prayer is the most essential weapon in the work of our salvation. But he who takes hold of it must expect temptations and be prepared for an inner battle, a battle with thoughts. The demons do not like the Jesus Prayer and in every way they take vengeance on the person who strikes them with this sword.

St. Barsanuphius

One should not pay attention to tempting thoughts, but should drive them far away from himself, and not being disturbed, continue the mental work. Though the fruit of this labor be imperceptible, though a person may not experience spiritual delights, tenderness, etc.—still prayer cannot remain inactive. It quietly completes its work.

St. Barsanuphius

SILENCE

Be more silent. But if they ask you something, even in church, answer them without being irritated, without having a sullen appearance.

St. Barsanuphius

Remember the monastic rule—do not begin a conversation yourself, not being asked something.

St. Nikon

Silence prepares a soul for prayer. Stillness—how beneficially it acts upon a soul!

St. Nikon

Maintain silence among you. Say only what is necessary and nothing extraneous, so that your mind will be pure for prayer. Reproach yourself mentally, disparage yourself, and consider yourself to be worse than everyone, and God will see your humility and will shield you from all temptations.

St. Moses

Silence is beneficial for the soul. When we talk it is difficult to refrain from idle talking and judging others. But there is also a bad silence, when someone is angry and for this reason is silent.

St. Nikon

The Kingdom of God is not in words but in deed. One should speak less, keep silence more, not judge anyone, to everyone my respect.

St. Ambrose

MONASTICISM

Concerning monastic life, one must, not seven times, but seventy times consider it well; and then, already once and for all, decide to enter a holy monastery for the monastic life.

St. Anthony

In order to live in a monastery, one needs not a wagon full of patience, but a whole wagon train.

St. Ambrose

Monasticism is an image of humility, and until they acquire it, monastics experience a multitude of battles and temptations for which one should prepare himself; but the Lord is powerful to strengthen us.

St. Macarius

There is external and internal monasticism. One cannot disregard the external, but one also cannot be satisfied with that alone. The external side without the internal will even bring harm. External monasticism one can liken to plowing the earth. As much as you may plow, nothing will grow if you do not sow anything. Internal monasticism is the sowing—while the millet is the Prayer of Jesus. Prayer illuminates the entire inner life of a monk and gives him strength in the battle. It is especially essential in enduring sorrows and temptations.

St. Barsanuphius

In order to be a nun, one must be a little iron, a little gold.... Iron—that means to have great patience, gold—great humility.

St. Ambrose

Monasticism is blessedness which is possible only for a person on earth. There is nothing higher than this blessedness. And this is because monasticism gives the key to inner life. Blessedness is within us, one must merely open it. Complete blessedness is in heaven, in the future life it only continues.

St. Barsanuphius

If a monk resides in a house in the world, they regard him like a layman. A monk cannot live in the world for long. Like a fish out of water, so is a monk out of his monastery.

St. Nikon

Our monastic work: to humble ourselves, to bow, and to beg forgiveness—by this we are justified.

St. Nikon

In our times God does not send the ascetics such trials as in ancient times, for they could not bear them, and He does not grant the gifts as in ancient times, so that they do not become excessively conceited.

St. Leo

Guard the conscience, maintain peace, labor according to your strength, pray always: be like a nun at all times, while walking, lying down, and eating, and the Lord will abide with you for always.

St. Anatoly

Monasticism itself has a great spiritual importance, and brings great spiritual benefit to those who approach it with a sincere attitude and live the life with simplicity and gentleness in humility.

St. Ambrose

COURAGE

Genuine holy courage is always united with the feeling of deep humility. A humble person is always ready to endure everything, both internal and external, considering himself to be deserving not only of the sorrows which are sent to him, but even more. It is impossible to upset and confuse a humble person—he is ready for everything, as St. Moses the Black said when they drove him out of the trapeza: *I made ready, and I was not troubled* (Ps. 118:60). And so, let us prepare our souls and hearts with humility, and it will help us to endure every temptation.

St. Nikon

INSTRUCTION

Direct your younger brother skillfully, first with prayer for him, and then with brief advice, putting everything in the Lord's hands, for it is by Him that the steps of man are made straight. Watch over yourself wherever you may be.

St. Moses

INGRATITUDE

If you do good, you must do it only for God. For this reason you must pay no attention to the ingratitude of people. Expect a reward not here, but from the Lord in heaven. If you expect it here—it will be in vain and you will endure deprivation.

St. Ambrose

DISBELIEF

Stubborn disbelief and denial of the existence of God—despite obvious miracles performed, despite a multitude of facts irrefutably proving the existence of God—is called unforgivable blasphemy against the Holy Spirit, leading to perdition. Stubborn denial and disbelief are blasphemy against the Spirit of God, are not forgiven either in this life or the next one, and a person who dies in his disbelief, not having repented, has perished.

St. Barsanuphius

NONBELIEVERS

One may have a good worldly relationship with nonbelievers, but one cannot have a relationship in prayer and one must not carry on arguments about religion so that the name of God not be offended during an argument.

St. Nektary

INFIRMITIES

Seeing one's own infirmities, one can judge condescendingly concerning the infirmities of others.

St. Macarius

With bodily infirmities, you must adapt yourself to them; to force yourself even more could completely disable you, only you must arm yourself against laziness.

St. Macarius

INSENSITIVITY

If at one end of the village they will be hanging people, at the other end they won't stop sinning, saying; "They won't reach us for some time yet."

St. Ambrose

PROMISE

An unfulfilled promise is just like a good tree without fruit.

St. Ambrose

CAUTION IN SPEECH

During conversation with others it is no hindrance to be cautious in speech, and at the same time one can retain the Jesus Prayer in the mind.

St. Hilarion

CONDEMNATION

One must remember the words of the Lord Himself in the Gospel: *I will have mercy and not sacrifice* (Matt. 9:13), i.e., in order to please the Lord one must most of all take care not to condemn others, and in general have an indulgent disposition towards his neighbors.

St. Ambrose

By the purity of our thoughts we can see everyone as holy and good. When we see them as fools, this comes from our frame of mind.

St. Macarius

Having received help or having improved for the better, beware of thoughts that praise you but condemn others. This is a trap of the enemy, beckoning you to arrogance and taking away all the fruits of virtue.

St. Macarius

You should be attentive to your inner life so as not to notice what is happening around you. Then you will not judge.

St. Ambrose

Do not judge others, for this alone will intercede for us during any judgement before God.

St. Macarius

Before God, a repentant sinner is more beloved than a conceited righteous person. And therefore beware of judging!

St. Anatoly

As soon as condemnation comes into your head, immediately say with attention: "Lord, grant me to see my sins and not condemn my brother".

St. Nektary

One must not condemn anyone, even the most wretched sinner.

St. Nikon

The Lord sees the hearts of men. But in their judgements people can always be mistaken, and then these judgements become the fruit of simple idle talking.

St. Nikon

As soon as you condemn someone, say to yourself: *Thou hypocrite, first cast the beam out of thine own eye* (Matt. 7:5).

The beam in the eye is pride. The Pharisee had all the virtues, but he was proud; the Publican, however, had humility, and was better.

St. Ambrose

Have pity, and you will not condemn.

St. Anatoly

Righteous judgement must relate to us ourselves, but not to others, and not according to our outward actions must we judge ourselves, but according to our inner condition or feeling.

St. Ambrose

You must firmly remember this spiritual law of life: if you condemn someone for something or are disturbed by something in another person, you will experience the very same thing. You will do that which you condemned someone else for doing, or you will suffer from the same infirmity.

St. Nikon

Humility, patience, and not judging others are needful everywhere. A peaceful state of soul is acquired only with these spiritual means, in proportion to the amount that we strive for humility, long-suffering, and non-condemnation of others.

St Ambrose

The main thing that is required of every person—do not judge anyone. It seems simple, but begin to fulfill it and it seems difficult. The enemy violently attacks a person and suggests to him thoughts of judging. The Lord says, "Forgive," while the enemy suggests, "Take vengeance on the offender. He's reviling you, you revile him." You should not listen to the enemy, but must struggle against him.

St. Barsanuphius

Do not start examining the deeds of people, do not judge, do not say: "Why is it this way? What is this for?" It is better to say to yourself, "What does their work have to do with me? I will not answer for them at the Dread Judgement of God." Divert every thought of yours from judging the deeds of people, and pray fervently to the Lord that He help you in this, because without the help of God we can do nothing good, as the Lord Himself said: *Without Me you can do nothing* (John 15:5).

St. Ambrose

Never condemn anyone. Greet everyone with a good disposition, whoever he may be, with the hope of finding in him only good, seeing before you the image of God.

St. Nikon

Some people are prone to the sin of condemnation due to habit, others from remembering wrongs, others from envy and hatred, but for the most part, we are prone to this sin due to conceit and haughtiness. In spite of our incorrigibility and sinfulness, it still seems to us that we are better than many others. If we desire to be corrected of this sin of condemnation, we must in every way force ourselves to be humble before God and man and implore God for help in this.

St. Ambrose

RELATIONS WITH NEIGHBORS

With all the people you meet on the path of life, behave as you would like them to behave with you.

St. Nikon

One cannot live without patience and complaisance towards one's neighbor.

St. Nikon

If someone is upset with you (i.e., not at peace with you, but does not express it), be pleasant with him, as if you don't notice it.

St. Ambrose

Discord destroys people.

St. Nikon

We should not give free reign to our feelings. We should behave affably towards those with whom we are not pleased.

St. Nikon

You should be respectful of everyone. Be friendly, but not too friendly. Make a bow and quickly pass by.

St. Ambrose

If some sort of misunderstanding occurs among us, or it seems that they are doing something bad intentionally, then we must immediately explain ourselves. Then every misunderstanding will vanish.

St. Nikon

Be silent before everyone and they will all love you.

St. Ambrose

Regard everyone with simplicity.

St. Ambrose

Our salvation and our ruin—is in our neighbor. Our salvation depends on how we relate to our neighbor. Do not forget to see the image of God in your neighbor.

St. Nikon

He who yields, receives three and a half measures, and he who decides to admonish and correct, receives only one measure, and sometimes he does not receive even that, when he gets upset and upsets the other person.

St. Ambrose

You should not oppose and struggle against people who cause evil, not only by word and deed, but even in your thoughts. Otherwise the demons will be victorious. You should pray for such people. Then the Lord will help and the demons will withdraw. A monk must prepare for death; therefore you must think about meeting death, at peace with everyone.

St. Nikon

The first and most essential means of making peace with those who offend and persecute us is to pray for them according to the commandment of Christ.

St. Leo

One should not be angry at others to the point of remembrance of wrongs. In accord with the commandment of the Lord, force yourself to pray for all those who hate and offend you!

St. Anatoly

Live in a Godly manner. Be meek and merciful toward the sisters, remembering God as much as you can, and you will be saved.

St. Anatoly

It is helpful for us to always remember how Blessed Theodora reasoned when she was ill treated, saying to herself, "you are unworthy of the love of your neighbors."

St. Ambrose

We should and must take special care that our self-indulgence does not hinder the salvation of our neighbor, his spiritual peace and spiritual progress. For this, we will give a full account to God, if we are not careful. It is the Christian duty to help in the salvation of our neighbor, not impede it.

St. Ambrose

One must strive to have a good opinion of everyone. Only God is the Knower of hearts. We cannot infallibly judge people.

St. Hilarion

DESPAIR

One must first of all abstain from sin and avoid occasions leading to it, but by no means must one despair, for despair deprives one of the hope of salvation, causes one to fall into greater sins, and is considered by God to be the most grievous sin.

St. Macarius

Despair is a mortal sin. Flee from it. And believe in the Merciful God, our Mediatrix the Theotokos and the Saints. They can do all things. But it is absolutely necessary to humble oneself and be patient.

St. Anatoly

One should not despair of Divine mercy in any situation, given the example of the harlot, the thief, and the publican in the Gospel, who repented and received forgiveness from the Merciful Lord.

St. Anatoly

SINFUL FALLS

Our falls into anger and other movements of the passions demonstrate to us our underlying spiritual pride and they humble us against our will; if we strive to eradicate this root, the branches will fall off by themselves.

St. Macarius

Much experience is needed before we truly realize our infirmity and are humbled, and this is acquired not quickly, but with much time. Our falls themselves bridle our arrogance and humble us against our will. But before God it is better to be a sinner with repentance than a righteous man with pride.

St. Macarius

Falling and rising, repenting and being humbled is better than not falling, not repenting and not being humbled; from the battle we learn skill.

St. Macarius

REMEMBRANCE OF WRONGS

You must force yourself, even against your will, to do some kind of good for your enemies, but mainly—do not take revenge on them; and be careful not to offend them with a scornful and disparaging look.

St. Ambrose

REMEMBRANCE OF DEATH

We must not be carefree, but we must beware that death not visit our cell unexpectedly. Therefore let us pray and watch, for blessed are the servant and the handmaid whom death finds watching, and unworthy and cursed are they whom it finds being slothful and immersed in carelessness (as in sleep), concerning the salvation of their poor souls.

St. Anthony

Strive to be always prepared for death, for death is near to both the elderly and the young, to monks and laymen equally, and often it comes suddenly and unexpectedly. Let everyone consider what will happen with his soul.

St. Barsanuphius

Remembrance of death teaches us to be attentive to ourselves. Often in the blossoming years they are carried away from this life to the eternal, and it is more terrifying if it is sudden. And we who are nearing the doors of the tomb, can we prolong our life for many years? Let us repent and we will live spiritually forever.

St. Leo

In order to awaken us from our negligence we must always bring to mind that we are mortal, our life passes by very quickly and is very perilous because the hour of our death is unknown, for although we know that we will die, we do not know when: whether today, or tomorrow, whether early or late, during the day or at night. This fate of every man is entirely unknown, when the scythe of death will reap someone, and in what state it will find him: ready with good deeds, or not ready and overflowing

with evil deeds. In whatever state it finds someone, that is how he will stand in judgement before God, and by his deeds each one will either be glorified or put to shame. And no one will come to our aid before God at that hour of death, only our good deeds.

St. Moses

MOVING TO ANOTHER MONASTERY

A place does not save you. There is no place where you can flee from yourself.

St. Nikon

Wherever we may decide to withdraw to or resettle, we will drag along our inner chaos, for just as everywhere is an earthly paradise for humble souls, for the proud everywhere will be torture and hard labor, worse than death. Do not assume that you will have quiet outside your monastery, but seek it in the spirit of humility of Christ and within your own heart, reproaching yourself in all things and with all your soul considering yourself to be unworthy of practicing stillness.

St. Anthony

SORROW

If you desire to be delivered from sorrow, do not let your heart be attached to anything or anyone. Sorrow comes from attachments to visible things.

St. Nikon

There never was and there never will be a place on earth free from sorrows. The only sorrowless place possible is the heart, when the Lord is present there.

St. Nikon

In difficulties, misunderstandings, and in all situations our nearest and most reliable recourse is only turning to the Lord and submitting to Him all our sorrows and cares. At the same time one should pray to God for all those involved in the matter, and everything will turn out well. The Lord enlightens every man who comes into the world and gives peace to our souls. Despondency and sorrow are useless in a matter requiring courage.

St. Moses

If there is no one to whom you can reveal your soul, tell your sorrow to the Lord God.

St. Nikon

It is harmful to sorrow excessively and inappropriately chastise oneself, but in all things one must thank the Lord for all things, however He might punish us with afflictions in this world.

St. Leo

ASCETICISM

Do not grow despondent in the battle of thoughts waged against you by the unseen enemy of our souls; even if you suffer a thousand wounds in a day, do not retreat from the struggle, cutting off your own will and understanding. God is good and merciful, and does not allow temptations beyond your measure, but this is needful and helpful for your instruction. Consider yourself to be the least among men.

St. Macarius

It is better, seeing your poverty, to always reproach yourself and fall down before the Lord with humility, rather than look at your improvement. Maintain the middle, humble path, and do not ascend prematurely to a higher path, beyond your strength. Seeing your own (spiritual) poverty, do not reproach anyone, do not condemn, consider yourself to be the very least, and when you receive reproach and scorn from someone, consider yourself to be worthy of it.

St. Macarius

Only a few physically strong persons can live a severe way of life, enduring cold, hunger, dampness, and lying on the ground. But according to St. John of Damascus, for those who are physically weak, humility and thanksgiving are more beneficial than bodily labors and struggles for which they are not suited.

St. Ambrose

Bodily struggles and labors are required only of those who are physically strong; humility with thanksgiving are more beneficial for the weak. Humility can take the place of physical labors, which without humility do not bring any kind of benefit.

St. Ambrose

SUSPICION

Flee from suspicion like fire, for with it the enemy of the human race catches people in his net and strives to present everything in a distorted appearance—white is black and black is white, as he did in Paradise with our ancestors Adam and Eve.

St. Ambrose

REPENTANCE

The foundation of our salvation is repentance.

St. Nikon

Years are not needed for true repentance, and not days, but only an instant.

St. Ambrose

Repentance is sincere only when a person, feeling his sins by which he angered his Creator, ceases from his sinful actions, grieves over them, repents, and is made worthy of forgiveness by the grace of Christ through absolution from a priest of the Church. However, when he does not cease from sinning, even though he is sorry, then this is not repentance, but rather a dangerous, excessive, and foolish hope in the goodness of God which, like despair, will be equally condemned before God.

St. Macarius

Repentance is true when afterwards you are strengthened in order to strive to live as you should; without this it is ineffectual, if you repent only to talk about your sins, but continue living as before.

St. Joseph

We must always prepare for death with repentance, whose efficacy is measured not by the quantity of prostrations but by heartfelt zeal. Remember that *a sacrifice unto God is a broken spirit: a heart that is broken and humble God will not despise* (Ps. 50:19). Therefore, when you do not fulfill your rule, due to bodily weakness or for some other reason, substitute this deficiency with self-reproach and humility.

St. Macarius

Hurry to expose your spiritual wounds before the Lord and seek absolution and forgiveness. And if after forgiveness you again fall into sins, again flee to repentance, and so on until the end. And God, seeing your labor, your repentance, will not leave you without His help and mercy. If He commanded us to forgive a repentant brother seventy times seven, will He not grant us even more forgiveness when we flee to Him with repentance? The fact that passions do not diminish—this is according to the providence of God. The holy fathers write that passions and falls humble a person, lead him to heartfelt compunction, and thereby attract to him Divine mercy.

St. Joseph

Have a general feeling of repentance. Have humility. Endure everything that the Lord sends you, and He, the Merciful One, will accept your repentance and will have mercy on you.

St. Nikon

In the words of self-praise and self-justification there is always concealed recalcitrance and pride, which God abhors. After sinning one must "flee"—you say, "where to?" To the quiet harbor of heartfelt repentance. Each night before you go to sleep recount to God, the Knower of hearts, all of your transgressions, committed in deed, word, and thought, and have faith that God will accept your heartfelt repentance. At the same time strive to humble your heart by reminding yourself that death can come unexpectedly.

St. Joseph

A trait of true repentance is that it opens your eyes to your sinfulness and to sin in general.

St. Nikon

It is not surprising to fall, but to remain in sin is shameful and arduous.

St. Ambrose

With all our might we must flee and avoid sin; but if because of our carelessness we fall into sin, we only deserve greater condemnation. But when we happen to sin involuntarily or due to our weakness, let us purify ourselves with repentance. Flee from pride, for it is the cause of many terrible falls. Humble yourself, reproach yourself, consider yourself to be the least, and worse than everyone, do not condemn anyone, and then you will receive Divine mercy.

St. Joseph

The reviving of a soul is performed by the will and power of God, but for this the consent and will of a person is required in offering repentance to God. The amount of repentance required from a sinner is known only to God. The repentant sinner, being ever forgotten by God, as it seems to him, obtains profit through the wondrous providence of God, and makes progress.

St. Nikon

God will judge our repentance not according to our labors, but according to our humility. On that day God will judge us not according to how many psalms we read, not for the prayers we did not say (or prayer rules we did not perform), but because we did not repent! There is great joy with the Angels in Heaven over one repentant sinner. Let us pray: "Lord have mercy. Lord grant me humility and meekness." Or: "By the judgements which Thou knowest, save me, O Lord!" And according to His mercy, the Lord will have mercy and will save all of us by His Grace.

St. Joseph

Every day and every hour begin your correction anew, and the God of mercy, compassion, and love for mankind will extend to us His hand to help, as He did to the Holy Apostle Peter who was drowning in the waves of the sea.

St. Joseph

The details of the confession are not important, but the compunction of the heart. "The Lord sees the heart".

St. Nektary

You should always offer repentance to the Lord for your carelessness and force yourself to fulfill the commandments of the Lord and your monastic vows. At the same time you should reproach yourself for your carelessness and consider yourself to be worse and more sinful than everyone, and humble yourself in your heart before the Lord. Humility takes the place of insufficient works.

St. Joseph

One can divide all of mankind into two parts: pharisees and publicans. The former will perish, the latter will be saved. Guard the consciousness of your sinfulness. This is very valuable before the Lord. What saved the Publican? Of course, it was the consciousness of his sinfulness: "Lord, be merciful to me, a sinner!" Behold, this prayer has been passed on now for two thousand years. But notice, the Publican recognizes himself to be a sinner, but at the same time he hopes in the mercy of God. Without hope, one cannot be saved.

St. Barsanuphius

If when you sin, you turn immediately to God in repentance—this is very good. And so you must. And the Lord forgives. But afterwards tell your spiritual father or elder about it—if it is a serious sin.

St. Anthony

One should daily, before going to sleep, remember the sins committed during the day, and repent of them before the Lord.

St. Nikon

Only with the Lord and in the Lord can you find spiritual peace for yourself. Your tormented soul can find comfort only in the Lord, in repentance and the correction of your life. With its poison, sin kills the soul of man. The soul resurrects from the life-giving action of repentance..

St. Nikon

The All-good Lord requires nothing from us except sincere repentance, and through it He leads those who repent to His eternal Heavenly Kingdom: *Repent, for the Kingdom of Heaven is at hand* (Matt. 3:2).

St. Ambrose

The success and joy of a monk are in the recognition of his sinfulness, in seeing his sins. One should base all of one's actions, life, and behavior in complete agreement with the recognition and knowledge of one's sinfulness. Seeing one's sins is a gift of God. One should ask for it from God.

St. Nikon

In case of a fall of some kind in deed, word, or thought, you should immediately repent and, acknowledging your infirmity, humble yourself and force yourself to see your sins, but not your corrections. From examining his sins, a person comes to humility and acquires a heart that is broken and humble, which God does not despise.

St. Hilarion

What a time we have come to! Before, if a person sincerely repented of his sins, he would change his sinful life for the better; but it happens that a person will describe all of his sins in detail during confession, and then he again goes and commits them.

St. Ambrose

Sins are like walnuts—you split open the shell, but the meat is hard to extract.

St. Ambrose

If someone happens to slip and fall accidently, involuntarily, he will be healed through repentance, tears, and acknowledgement of his infirmity, if in the future he does not give up fighting with himself, with the sin battling against us. If such a person falls—he will arise and will stand on his original course, not having sold himself to sin.

St. Nikon

A repentant sinner is more pleasing to God than a person who has not sinned, but is haughty. It is better having sinned, to repent, than not sinning and to be proud of it. The Pharisee refrained from sin, but for being puffed up and condemning the Publican, he was deprived of his righteousness before God; but the Publican, having sinned greatly, through the humble acknowledgement of this and enduring the reproaches of the Pharisee, received not only the forgiveness of sins, but he surpassed the justification of the Pharisee.

St. Ambrose

Everyone not only may, but they must be concerned about pleasing God. But how does one please Him? First of all, through repentance and humility.

St. Ambrose

One should merit remission of sins through repentance and tears, and implore God to grant mercy at His Terrible Judgement. It is better to be punished here than to be assigned to eternal torment there, justly deserved for our daily sins.

St. Joseph

Do not let the enemy, the devil, deceive us! If anyone sees that he is stuck fast in sin, that sin has gained great power over him, taking advantage of his forgetfulness and lack of understanding, that he has sailed far off into the sea of sin and that the way back to God is long and difficult—let him not despair; he only needs the sincere desire to return to God, and He is already waiting for us.

St. Nikon

REST

When you want to receive true spiritual rest, then listen to the Lord who has commanded us: *learn of Me; for I am meek and lowly in heart: and ye shall have rest unto your souls* (Matt. 11:29). See what the Lord especially commands us to learn—humility and meekness, which only can give us rest, but this science is mastered not all at once, and not in one day or one year, but with much time, forcing oneself and Divine help.

St. Macarius

To not have any sorrows and suddenly receive tranquility—in no way is this possible. When we conquer all the passions, exterminate pride and acquire humility, then we will find rest, for the Lord commanded us to learn from Him meekness and humility, in order to obtain rest (Matt. 11:29).

St. Macarius

In condemning others, we imagine ourselves to be someone of importance and we are deprived of peace; you know the words of the Lord: *Learn of Me, for I am meek and lowly in heart: and ye shall find rest unto your souls* (Matt. 11:29). So if we do not have spiritual peace it means that we do not have humility and meekness.

St. Macarius

Peace and tranquillity is a great reward, but if soldiers receive rewards for heroism and the shedding of blood, then we also—spiritual soldiers—must first of all endure many temptations and sorrows with humility, accuse ourselves and not others, and having thereby lessened our passions, i.e., conquered them, but most of all pride, arrogance, anger, rage, etc., we will then be worthy of this reward—spiritual peace.

St. Macarius

We seek peace, but it is not to our benefit. Rest is obtained on the cross and in turning ourselves over to the will of God. As long as we are battling the passions and are poorly armed against them, then it is impossible to acquire peace.

St. Macarius

HELP OF GOD

Falls usually happen through God's allowance so that we can recognize our human frailty. We cannot do any kind of good works without the help of God, and when it seems that we have done something pleasing to God, then because of this very thought, the work is already not pleasing to God.

St. Leo

Do not despair! The Lord is near. Declare to Him all of your sorrows and confusion. When human means are insufficient for understanding, then God's help immediately grants beneficial thoughts, when we turn to Him as children to a father.

St. Moses

The Lord begins to reveal His power when a person sees that all human means for providing help to the person in need are feeble.

St. Ambrose

No matter how many waves rise up in your soul, always flee to Christ. The Saviour will come to help and will calm the waves. Believe that the Lord has providentially arranged your life for your healing; do not reject it and do not seek bodily rest and imagined peace. It is necessary rather to be shaken and endure much. If you will have a revelation, it will greatly ease your battle and you will have more peace than just by yourself.

St. Leo

Do not be greatly disturbed by the arrangement of your fate. Have only the unwavering desire for salvation and, standing before God, await His help until the time comes.

St. Ambrose

HELP OF THE SAINTS

When you will say, "All Saints, pray to God for me!"—then all of the saints in heaven will cry out, " Lord have mercy!"—and you will have what you desire.

St. Nektary

THOUGHTS

The thoughts that vex and annoy us have many distinctions: a provocation, or an attack of a thought, is not a sin but is a test of our free will, to what it is inclined—to the thought or to opposition of it. However, when there is agreement and communion with these passions it is considered to be a sin and repentance is needed. He who does not have the strength to oppose them himself must hasten to God, cast down his infirmity and implore His help and the help of the Mother of God. When someone is conquered by thoughts, it is a sign that pride preceded them, and therefore he must humble himself more.

St. Macarius

Do not be confused because dark thoughts often trouble you, for dark thoughts, like autumn clouds, come one after another and darken everything. But then they pass and the sky remains clear and pleasant. And so our thoughts wander, they wander around the wide world, but the mind remains planted in its place, and then it is quiet, and the soul becomes joyful. But our mind, from wandering here and there, becomes accustomed to the brief but often repeated Prayer of Jesus, which may God grant you the habit of saying, and then your days will be bright.

St. Anthony

To guard one's soul from thoughts—this is a difficult matter, the significance of which is not even comprehensible to worldly people. They often say: "Why guard the soul from thoughts? Well, a thought came and then it left; why battle with it?" They are very much mistaken. A thought does not simply come and go. One thought destroys the soul of a person, another thought compels a person to reverse his course of life and go in a direction completely different from previously. The holy fathers say that there are thoughts from God, thoughts from ourselves, i.e., from our nature, and thoughts from demons. In order to determine the source of the thoughts—are they inspired by God or the enemy power, or do they come from nature—requires great wisdom.

St. Barsanuphius

Agreement with sinful thoughts is communion with the enemy, from which Divine power and help departs from us.

St. Nikon

When having thoughts of self-praise, we must look at our sins and remember that without the help of God we can do nothing good and beneficial; we have only sins and infirmities.

St. Hilarion

Our invisible enemy himself plants a sinful thought in the soul of a person, and then records it as if it were the person's own thought, so that later he can accuse the person at the terrible judgement of God.

St. Ambrose

Reveal all your thoughts, especially those which will not leave you alone.

St. Barsanuphius

The Lord will deliver you from all improper thoughts; just humble yourself.

St. Ambrose

Do not be surprised that various thoughts arise during the time of the services: when you take up arms against the enemies, i.e., prayer, then they arm themselves against you more forcefully with provocative thoughts. Flee to the Lord with prayer against them and do not become confused: they will vanish. When you become confused, seeing that they do not leave you, they arm themselves even more against you; but when you chant unto God with humility, then you will be at peace.

St. Macarius

Sometimes they leave church because of thoughts. This, of course, is foolish. The enemy begins the attack of thoughts with the purpose of driving them from church. We must not surrender to the enemy. In most cases, the young ones have lustful thoughts, while the older ones have thoughts of anger, remembering past offenses. The enemy might say: "Remember how so and so insulted you in front of everyone, and you were silent and didn't say a word to him. Come on! This is what you should have told him..." Sometimes from similar thoughts someone will completely flare up in anger. One must battle the thoughts.

St. Barsanuphius

When thoughts disturb, confuse, or worry you, you should not converse with them, but simply say: "May the will of God be done!" This is very calming.

St. Barsanuphius

If we become engrossed in filthy thoughts—let us not despair, but let us quickly hasten to the pure water of repentance and self-reproach, and the Merciful Lord will forgive.

St. Anatoly

You cannot live without having thoughts. Still, without manure you will not grow any grain. They braid a crown for the wise person. Give opportunity to a wise man and he will become even wiser. But whoever is being braided by them (the thoughts), let him repent, arise, and be saved.

St. Anatoly

Transient thoughts to which the heart does not become attached quickly pass by, like in a kaleidoscope. Our mind never stops; it is always busy. You should not consider foolish thoughts to be our inalienable property. They are not from our nature. One and the same mind cannot both glorify and blaspheme God. You should not pay such thoughts any attention, but throw them away like trash, like something extraneous.

St. Nikon

If some kind of foolish thought continually comes to mind and the heart attaches to it and sympathizes with it, then one must apply all of his strength to drive it away, with the help of the Jesus Prayer and confession to the elder.

St. Nikon

We must never dwell on thoughts. Let them pass by. If they come to us, drive them off with the Jesus Prayer. Let them not find any sympathy in our hearts. Strive to cleanse your heart. For this it is necessary to have, besides the Jesus Prayer, the memory of God, and a careful and frank confession.

St. Nikon

When you notice that some thought is repeatedly coming to you and your heart is becoming attached to it, then you are in terrible danger; you must quickly fight to drive it away. Chase it off with the Jesus Prayer, but if you do not have the strength, then confess it to your elder.

St. Nikon

The Lord waits: where will our heart be inclined—to preserve faithfulness to Him or betray Him for the temporary sweetness of sin. The holy fathers have said: "Cut off the thought, and you cut off everything." It is very important to remember that with every agreement with sin, and through sin with the demons, we betray the Lord, we betray Him for the loathsome price of sin. Whom and for what are we bartering?! Personally not consenting to sin and struggling against it with prayer and confession are absolutely necessary.

St. Nikon

Contrast your proud and self-confident thoughts about perfection with extreme humility before God and men, reproaching yourself that you haven't even learned oral prayer and do not fulfill your cell rule. From where has this perfection suddenly appeared?

St. Ambrose

During prayer you must strive to reject all thoughts and, not paying them any attention, continue the prayer. If the attack of thoughts greatly increases, again you must implore God's help against them.

St. Ambrose

The means to fight lustful thoughts: humility, self-reproach, abstinence, but more than anything else—love for your neighbor—for the weak, the infirm, the sick, and those bound by the passions.

St. Anatoly

The most serious battles are with thoughts of lust and despair. One must humble himself. Humility attracts the help of God. The corrupting effect of lustful thoughts comes from enjoying them—divine grace withdraws for a long time. One can attract it back again only through sincere repentance and the rejection of these thoughts.

St. Nikon

Humble yourself before those younger than you, practice self-denial, do not eat to satiety, for from this the thoughts greatly increase. If you behave boldly and willfully, you will not escape the cruel battle of the flesh.

St. Joseph

When lustful thoughts afflict you, make as many prostrations as you can. Without doing battle, not one soul has entered Paradise. And the victors are crowned.

St. Anatoly

Against impure thoughts use the spiritual sword—the name of God. You must offer repentance to the Lord, and you must not hide anything from your spiritual father. Wounds that are exposed heal quickly.

St. Joseph

The holy fathers in general consider blasphemous thoughts to be not our thoughts but provocations of the enemy; and when we do not agree with them but grieve that they have penetrated our mind, then this is a sign that we are not guilty of them. One should not be disturbed that they come. When a person becomes disturbed, the enemy attacks him even more, but when he pays no attention, disregards them and does not consider them to be a sin, then the thoughts vanish.

St. Macarius

Doubts, just like lustful and blasphemous thoughts, should be despised and not paid any attention. Despise them and the enemy, the devil, will not endure, but will depart from you, for he is proud and will not endure scorn. But if you enter into conversation with them—for all lustful, blasphemous, and doubting thoughts are not yours—then they will overcome you, knock you down, and finish you.

St. Barsanuphius

You must scorn doubting, blasphemous and lustful thoughts; then they will not harm you in any way, especially if you reveal them to your elder. But you should not reveal them in detail, otherwise you can harm both yourself and your elder. You should especially cover up lustful thoughts, cover this stinking cesspool with a curtain and do not dig into it.

St. Barsanuphius

Do not be bothered by blasphemous thoughts, but try to despise them. God will not call you to account for them—they are from the devil.

St. Anatoly

Especially do not be disturbed by blasphemous thoughts which clearly come from the envy of the enemy. They occur in a person either because of proud self-opinion or the condemnation of others.

St. Ambrose

ABUSE

If they think you are proud because you are reclusive—rejoice. If they disturb your prayer, do not despair, but humble yourself.

St. Anatoly

OBEDIENCE

Obedience is what directs us on the path of perfection.

St. Macarius

When Christ the Saviour Himself was obedient, it was not for a brief period of time, but unto death. Therefore, if we are always obedient we will always be happy. But to our sorrow, the cruel passion of self-love has made our will iron, i.e., unbending to obedience: often it seems to us that we are smart, and that we can see things better than others can, etc.

St. Anthony

Genuine obedience which brings great benefit to the soul comes when you act in defiance of yourself. Then the Lord Himself takes you in His arms and blesses your labors.

St.Nikon

Take this advice for your whole life: if the superiors or those older than you suggest something, then no matter how difficult or how lofty it might seem, do not refuse. God will help you for your obedience.

St.Nektary

If the work of the redemption of mankind was performed by the obedience unto death of the incarnate Son of God to the Father, then every appointed position is nothing other than obedience to God, because the various kinds of offices are allocated by the Holy Spirit, as the Apostle Paul testifies (I Cor. 12:28).

St. Ambrose

Every obedience which seems difficult, becomes very easy when we fulfill it, because that is how obedience works.

St. Nektary

Go where they send you, look at what they show you, and say at all times: "Thy will be done!"

St. Ambrose

It is better to be a disciple of a disciple than to live according to your own will. In the writings of the holy fathers they talk about this. It is not shameful to obey the advice of your spiritual father, but rather salvific and indispensible; and he who does not listen to good advice will be punished.

St. Ambrose

Strive in all things to live according to the Divine commandments, and remember that the Lord is present and sees the disposition of your heart. While fulfilling an obedience, consider that it has been given by the Lord through a person, and that your salvation depends on your zeal in fulfilling it.

St. Ambrose

FASTING

While refraining from food, one must also refrain from the passions.

St. Macarius

The Holy Church cries out: fasting is not avoiding food, but putting away all evil, controlling the tongue from idle-talking and gossip, forbearing from anger, and abstaining from lust, falsehood, and flattery. Whoever fasts in this way, his fast is pleasing to God.

St. Anthony

One must absolutely keep the fasts on Wednesdays and Fridays and all Great Lent. Absolutely fast.

St. Anatoly

Refrain from food as much as possible and try to eat light and familiar foods in moderation.

St. Leo

The essence and power of abstinence is not in refraining from food, but in expelling from the heart every remembrance of evil and other such things. That is true fasting, and what above all else the Lord demands from us.

St. Leo

Fasting is praiseworthy and necessary in its time and place: it is better to keep to a moderate use of food and drink, avoiding satiety, indicated by a slight heaviness, and on the other hand, avoiding excessive and inappropriate abstinence. Moderation, the middle path, makes a person more capable of spiritual activity.

St. Ambrose

PRAISE

Whoever reproaches us, gives us a gift, but whoever praises us, steals from us.

St. Ambrose

How harmful is the praise of man! Even though a person may have done something worthy of praise, when he enjoys the sound of praise he is already deprived of future glory, according to the teachings of the holy fathers.

St. Macarius

To have a high opinion of oneself is a serious sin before God; but people afflicted with this not only do not repent of it, but they do not even consider it a sin. Flee from this evil root!

St. Macarius

If they will praise you, you must remain silent—do not say anything.

St. Ambrose

Pay no attention to praise and fear it; remember what one of the holy fathers says: "If someone praises you, expect reproaches from him too."

St. Hilarion

We must fear every kind of praise and glory from men, for according to the teachings of the holy fathers, "it is not only the one who accepts praise from men, but even the one who hears the sounds of the words with enjoyment, that is deprived of eternal glory." Lord, do not allow us to be carried away by the enjoyment of the vainglory of this world!

St. Macarius

A true monk does not reproach and does not praise.

St. Ambrose

JUSTICE

You need not strive for the justice of men; seek only Divine justice.

St. Nikon

RELIGIOUS FEAST DAYS

On feast days the enemy always tries to cause unpleasantness, sorrow. This one is struck, that one is insulted; he tries to give everyone something for the feast day. And the more attentive and strict you are with yourself, the more the enemy arms himself, and tries to treat you with something, especially on feast days. One must expect and be prepared for everything. But the Lord is merciful and on feast days He also distributes gifts. And you can receive something, but you notice it forty years later, perhaps. Then you realize what kind of gift the Lord sent you on that feast day.

St. Barsanuphius

The continuation of our life is the continuation of God's mercy to man, and therefore birthdays and name-days should be conducted not so much with noise and dissipated celebrations as much as with piety.

St. Anthony

Except out of extreme necessity one must never work on a feast day. You should value and honor a feast day. This day should be consecrated to God: you should go to church, pray at home, and read the Holy Scriptures and the works of the holy fathers, and do good deeds.

St. Nikon

IDLE TALKING

Flee conversations and every sin in general; but if you fall, repent and the Lord will help you and you will be more experienced and careful. Most importantly, never become confused.

St. Anatoly

Avoid joking and careless words in relations with one another. This garrulity and idle talking can turn into a habit.

St. Nikon

RECONCILIATION

If you reconcile your own heart towards someone who is angry at you, the Lord will tell his heart to reconcile with you.

St. Hilarion

NATURE

For one who has acquired the love and habit of examining his surroundings, life in nature is beneficial; it saves him from petty, one-sided thinking and imparts to him a broader vision, integrity, and depth.

St. Barsanuphius

COMMUNION

It is very salutary to nourish your soul with the Eternal and Holy Bread. If a person should die on the very day when he has communed of the Holy Mysteries, the Holy Angels will receive his soul into their hands, for the sake of the communion, and he will pass safely through the heavenly toll-gates.

St. Anthony

In the Mystery of Repentance, of Confession, the promissory notes are torn up, i.e., the record of our sins is destroyed; but communion of the true Body and Blood of Christ gives us the strength to be spiritually reborn.

St. Barsanuphius

After communion you should ask the Lord that you preserve the Gift worthily and that the Lord help you so that you do not turn backward, i.e., to your former sins.

St. Ambrose

If we partake of the Mysteries of the Body and Blood of Christ with faith and not condemnation, then all of the snares of our spiritual enemies who harass us will become ineffectual and useless. We partake without condemnation, firstly, when we approach the Mysteries with sincere and humble repentance and confession of our sins, with the firm resolve not to return to them, and secondly, when we approach without the remembrance of wrongs, having become reconciled in our heart with all those who have grieved us.

St. Ambrose

It is difficult to say whether it is better to partake of the Holy Mysteries of Christ occasionally, or more often. Zacchaeus received his dear Guest, the Lord, into his home with joy, and he did well. While the Centurion, in humility recognizing his unworthiness, decided not to receive Him, and he also did well. Their actions, although completely opposite, according to their motives are the same, and before the Lord they appeared equally virtuous. The essence of the matter is that one must worthily prepare himself for this great Mystery.

St. Nikon

VOLITION

The work of our salvation depends on our volition, on God's help, and on cooperation. But the latter will not follow if the first does not precede it.

St. Ambrose

DIVINE PROVIDENCE

Faith does not consist of merely believing in the existence of God, but also in His all-wise Providence which guides His creatures and arranges everything for the good; the times and the seasons are put in His power (Acts 1:7), and for each of us the limits of our life were determined before our existence, and without His will a bird does not fall nor does a hair of our head perish! (Matt 10:29; Luke 21:28).

St. Macarius

God cares and provides for us more than we ourselves. He arranges our salvation, but He also does not want us to seek it in worldly enjoyment, but in sorrows, difficulties, and sicknesses. Was it not with infirmity that our fathers and mothers entered the Kingdom of Heaven? Did they not reach it by the narrow and sorrowful path? They sorrowed, but they did not grow weary and become despondent and this served as a comfort for them during the most cruel sorrows, spiritual and physical. Through enduring them with perfect humility they received absolute peace and even spiritual gifts.

St. Macarius

The works of God are wondrous and unfathomable for our darkened minds, but as much as possible, we see from Scripture and our personal experiences that the Lord sends sicknesses, sorrows, deprivation, droughts, wars, and revolutions, either as punishment for our sins, or in anticipation, so that we do not fall into sins, or sometimes to test our faith. And so, we must bow in reverence before His all-wise Providence and give thanks for His ineffable mercy towards us.

St. Macarius

How would we know ourselves if no one caused us sorrow, and how would we acquire patience, and how would we be humbled? All of this does not happen without Divine Providence, but by His most wise supervision, each person is presented situations which can disturb and shake him, for testing his will and patience, so that he can see his infirmity and be humbled, or so that he can acquire the virtues of patience and love.

St. Macarius

For the most part, the meaning and benefit of an experience are recognized afterwards.

St. Nikon

We do not know the judgements of God. He does everything for good. We are bound to earthly blessings, but He wants to give us future blessings through brief earthly sickness.

St. Macarius

We must be certain that Divine Providence always cares for us and arranges everything for the good, even in situations opposing us.

St. Leo

The Lord arranges everything for our benefit and spiritual instruction, according to His mercy and wisdom, but we, due to our weakness and passionate habit, understand poorly, like infants.

St. Leo

There is no shortage of instructions for virtue and piety; let us just be zealous for this and the laziness of the evil servant will withdraw. However, everything leads us to the good. For those who love God all things work for good.

St. Moses

His all-embracing Providence extends over the whole world, but especially over each of us.

St. Macarius

SIMPLICITY

The Lord abides in simple hearts. Gold is everywhere and everywhere it shines through, no matter from what angle; but something else, no matter how much you work with it, it still is not gold.

St. Ambrose

Everything simple is closer to God, but the wise and exalted separate us from God.

St. Ambrose

Let us live more simply and God will have mercy on us.

St. Ambrose

FORGIVENESS

In the spiritual life something that is very good is explained wisely at the proper time. Ask for forgiveness at the proper time in order to reconcile your own soul and to give this opportunity to others as well. It is not in vain written in the psalms: *Seek peace and pursue it* (Ps.33:15).

St. Ambrose

Before you ask the Lord for forgiveness, you must yourself forgive. This is what it says in the Lord's Prayer.

St. Nikon

You must forgive with much humility, placing the blame on yourself—this is a necessary condition for forgiving offenses. External prostrations and words alone do not reconcile you, they do not touch the heart but are like an empty sound.

St. Nikon

THE PATH TO SALVATION

Our salvation, according to St. Peter Damascene, is located between fear and hope, so that we do not have self-confidence and do not despair, but with blessed hope in the mercy and help of God, we strive to conduct a life in fulfillment of the Divine commandments.

St. Ambrose

Without winter there would be no spring, without spring there would be no summer. Likewise in the spiritual life: a little consolation, after which we sorrow a little, and so the path of salvation gradually takes shape.

St. Anatoly

According to human reasoning, the path of salvation, it would seem, should be a smooth path, quiet and peaceful; but according to the words of the Gospel, this path is sorrowful, difficult, and narrow. The Lord said, *I came not to send peace on earth, but a sword* (Matt.10:34).

St. Ambrose

What does a person need in order to learn the ways of the Lord? A person needs to be meek and humble, and then the Lord Himself will teach him how to walk the way of the Lord.

St. Ambrose

Humble yourself with God's help, be meek, have no malice for your neighbor, prepare your soul to receive Divine instruction with a meek and good life, and the Lord Himself will teach you His ways.

St. Nikon

The earthly lot of man—sorrow, labor, sickness, struggle, sadness, doubt, confinement, deprivation of this or that, insult, confusion, the rising of the passions, the battle with them, victory or exhaustion, or hopelessness and the like. It is not in vain that the Prophet David said: *There is no peace in my bones in the face of my sins. (Ps.* 37:4).

St. Ambrose

If you wait for only agreeable conditions for salvation, then you will never begin a God-pleasing life.

St. Nikon

A person wants one thing, but he himself does something entirely different from what he wants. His mind wants one thing, but the senses demand something else. And a person sees this and feels sick about it, that everything is not right; he understands that it is turning out wrong, not as it should be, and he becomes despondent seeing that he is not succeeding in the battle against the passions, that his spiritual life is not going well. But no, one must not despair, one must be patient.

St. Nikon

The beginning of salvation consists in rejecting your own will and understanding and doing the will of God.

St. Ambrose

One should patiently force himself in every virtue for the sake of the Lord, watch soberly over all of his feelings, thoughts, and deeds, call to the Lord God for help, and come to humility and recognize that by his own efforts and without God's help a person will not accomplish anything. And when, finally, the vessel of the human soul and body is prepared, when the strings of his harp are attuned to all humility, patience, and piety... then the time will come, and wonderful singing will resound, and the beautiful and marvelous sounds of spiritual life will pour forth, and *many shall see, and shall fear, and shall hope in the Lord* (Ps. 39:4), for this ineffable singing comes from union with the Lord.

St. Nikon

May the Lord strengthen your soul and sow in your heart faith, hope, and charity, the greatest and most important virtues, for faith makes us believe, hope makes us have trust, and charity makes us love God. These three virtues are equally needed for our salvation and without these no one will be worthy of the joy of beholding God and no one can be saved.

St. Leo

If you show mercy in some way to someone, for this you will obtain mercy. If you suffer along with those who suffer, which does not seem to be a great thing, you will be numbered with the martyrs. If you forgive someone who offends you, for this not only will all of your sins be forgiven, but you will be a daughter of the heavenly father. If you pray from your heart, even a little bit, for your salvation, you will be saved. If you do not condemn a sinner, for this you will receive salvation. If you reproach yourself before God for the sins felt by your conscience, for this you will be justified. If you confess your sins before God, for this there is forgiveness and a reward. If you sorrow for your sins, or feel compunction, or weep, or sigh, then your sighs are not hidden from Him, for St. Simeon says that not even a tear-drop nor a part of a drop, are hidden from Him.

St. Moses

The Lord cares for the salvation of your soul more than you think. He will save you if you just turn to Him with humility and hope and do even what seems to be little. The Lord God greatly values even the little, if it is done for His sake.

St. Moses

From now on let us strive firmly to not divide the path of Christ into various branches, but to combine them into one main one: to love the Lord with our whole soul and to maintain peace and holiness with everyone, not thinking foolishly or suspiciously about anyone.

St. Ambrose

The mistake on our part is that we do not want to submit our will to the all-good Divine Providence, which indicates to us through circumstances the path beneficial to our soul. Instead we look for some sort of peaceful way for ourselves which exists only in dreams, and in reality is nowhere on earth. There will be rest not for everyone, but only for a few, when they sing: "With the saints give rest..."

St. Ambrose

We are all confused: can't we arrange our retirement in such a way? And in retirement we often think: if it weren't for this inconvenience, if not for these circumstances, if not for that contrary person, then perhaps it would be easier and more peaceful for me; but we forget that discomforts often come from within us, like evil thoughts. Where the passions lie, from there proceed all of our discomforts, disagreements, squabbling, and disorder. But may He Who came to save sinners overcome all of these, if we desire to repent, and become humbled and submissive.

St. Ambrose

Perfect virtue is opposed and resisted by various sorrows, temptations, obstacles, and most of all by people prompted by the enemy of our salvation. The enemy desires to hinder good intentions and he instills people of this world with hatred for the servants of God.

St. Nikon

Do not get lost in sorrow, do not seek lofty gifts, but conduct yourself with humility: *feel compunction upon your beds for what ye say in your hearts* (Ps. 4:5). Reproach yourself for your imperfections; this is better than your lofty improvements accompanied by conceit. As long as we remain in this war, we must neither be bold nor despair.

St. Macarius

The Godly-wise fathers teach us that it is always better to reproach ourselves and in every unpleasant situation to lay the blame on ourselves, and not on others. Then we will find rest and spiritual peace, and we will hold fast to the true path to salvation.

St. Ambrose

JOY

There is joy in frequent remembrance of God, as it is written: *I remembered God and I was gladdened* (Ps. 76:4).

St. Anthony

We must begin with thanksgiving for everything. The beginning of joy is to be content with your situation.

St. Ambrose

IRRITABILITY

Irritability, or the anger part of our tripartite soul, is not given in order to be angry at our neighbors, but in order to have zeal against sin. When we become enraged with our neighbors, we do this contrary to our nature. Irritability is strong in us because of pride.

St. Macarius

Irritability shows us our inner disposition which we must overcome with self-reproach, patience, love, not noticing the weaknesses of our neighbors and not condemning others. Sometimes, however, we are offended, and this, of course, is not without Divine Providence, in order to show us our infirmity and give the means for healing: struggle, resistance, and humility.

St. Macarius

To fight against irritation we have patience, self-reproach, and contemplation of the sufferings of Christ.

St. Macarius

You must make every effort to restrain yourself, so as not to acquire the unfortunate habit of losing your temper. This unbearable vice is not as noticeable in oneself as it is in others, and those who become angry over nothing are deserving of the fire of Gehenna.

St. Anthony

As soon as you notice in yourself any irritation, just say firmly, "Lord have mercy." With prayer we are purified from every defilement.

St. Nektary

SPIRITUAL UNDERSTANDING

We should not be attracted to ourself, thinking that we are better than others, but we must consider ourselves to be the last of all; in this consists spiritual understanding and spiritual instruction.

St. Macarius

Begin gradually, do not trust yourself, do not depend on your own understanding, reject your own will, and the Lord will give you true understanding.

St. Macarius

Unfortunately, everywhere now they talk and write so freely about religion, not constructively, but to cast doubts. Sensuality has seized control and the younger generation is more inclined to freedom and not bridling the senses, and they give their thinking free rein, even though it is darkened.

St. Macarius

With humility the mind is pleasing to God, but with pride it is rejected.

St.Macarius

ABSENT-MINDEDNESS

Gradually train yourself not to be so absent-minded. For this, try to listen attentively and catch the meaning of the readings and the singing. Also frequently remember death, the judgement of God, and eternal torments. And do not give freedom to your eyes. Gaze more at the holy icons; looking at people is harmful for your soul.

St. Joseph

DISCERNMENT

True understanding, or discernment, is obtained through humility, and humility through sorrows. According to St. Peter Damascene, he who flees from sorrows, flees from his own salvation.

St. Macarius

PARENTS

He who honors his father is cleansed of his sins, he who honors his father will enjoy his own children, and when he prays, his prayers will be heard. Honor your father so that his blessing will be upon you. Child, come to your father's aid in his old age, and if he loses his senses in some way do not scorn or reproach him with all your might, for the prayers of a father will not be forgotten by God; do not criticize your father.

St. Leo

COMPLAINING

God endures all the sins of man, but He does not leave a complainer without punishment.

St. Macarius

Watch out for complaining and faintheartedness, which worsen and increase sorrows.

St. Macarius

Complaining against God occurs mostly with people who are haughty or foolish.

St. Anthony

Especially beware of complaining, no matter who it is against. Complaining is worse and more harmful than anything else. It is more beneficial and peaceful to blame yourself at all times for everything, and not others. You must especially beware of complaining against Divine Providence which arranges everything good and beneficial for our souls through the Mother of God. But due to our faintheartedness, we often are foolishly disturbed and we grieve senselessly over something arranged for our spiritual benefit.

St. Ambrose

On whom will the Lord look favorably: only on the meek and the silent... Thy will be done, O Lord, on me a sinner. Rest is promised for us in the future life, but here on earth, labor and temptation. Blessed is the man who endures.

St. Moses

Whatever might happen to us does not happen without God's permission, as said by the Righteous Job: *as it seemed good to the Lord, so has it come to pass* (Job 1:21). And therefore like him we must endure unpleasant experiences in life and restrain ourselves from complaining, and not say: "Why is it this way, and not that way?"

St. Anthony

GUIDANCE

Humility is born from true obedience and the rejection of self-centered thoughts, when we do not trust ourselves in any way, and cutting off our will and understanding, we entrust them to others who are able to guide us.

St. Macarius

Not having anyone to nourish or guide your soul, you must instead read books and be nourished by them, while imploring God's help.

St. Macarius

SELF-LOVE

Let us look around carefully. Do we not confuse ourselves through self-love and self-centeredness? Shouldn't we rather, according to the apostolic commandment, lay aside all pride and run with patience the race that is set before us ?(Heb. 12:1)

St. Leo

Our self-love interferes and opposes every good deed of ours, spoils it and corrupts it, and it especially hinders the offering of pure prayer to God.

St. Ambrose

From egoism and self-love come all misfortunes. They do not like when others touch us and they get so stirred up

that you can't protect yourself from their thoughts. They produce disgusting thoughts, like locusts, that devour not only spiritual fruit, but the leaves and the root itself.

St. Ambrose

CONCEIT

Conceit—that subtle arrow of the devil—secretly wounds the heart and it's seed is subtly planted, so that little by little it grows into a pharisee, and later it succumbs to complete pride—but this is the demonic realm.

St. Macarius

Watch carefully so that the thieving thought does not creep in, which says that you live better and more attentively than others. It is so dangerous that you will not even notice how, from a poppy seed falling on the heart, it will grow into a giant pharisee, turn into complete arrogance and more. Before the Lord it is better to be a sinner with repentance than a righteous person with pride.

St. Macarius

Do not consider every proud suggestion and opinion about yourself to be a minor sin, but prostrate yourself before God, and ask for forgiveness and help in being delivered from it.

St. Macarius

If you were not subject to temptation, and without recognizing your infirmities you saw only your own improvements and placed your hope of salvation on them, then you could fall into extreme haughtiness and incurable deception; for when the enemy cannot conquer someone through passions and infirmities, then he places into the mind haughtiness and conceit, from which they fall into deception and the darkening of the mind.

St. Macarius

Beware of having exalted thoughts about yourself. For this the grace of God withdraws its help and we are handed over to the passions and (evil) spirits as punishment.

St. Macarius

Through obedience humility is achieved; we recognize our worth and we flee from conceit.

St. Macarius

SELF-SUFFICIENCY

Self-sufficiency closes ones spiritual eyes, and a person then sees something other than reality.

St. Nikon

You should think humbly about yourself and begin every action of yours with humility; but you must drive far away false humility, displayed in excusing your unwillingness and laziness to struggle: "How can we sinners do that? Those people were saints..." That is what you hear from those people who do not want to labor for their salvation. You can answer them: "Yes, that is true, but very often the saints were previously great sinners, and by struggling they became saints. Therefore, consider yourself a sinner, but force yourself to do good. There will be benefit from it." Self-justification is the root of evil.

St. Nikon

Seeking to justify oneself cannot pacify the conscience. It only confuses a person more.

St. Nikon

Do not blame someone else: the malice is within us.

St. Nikon

SELF-KNOWLEDGE

We cannot know ourselves other than through association with our neighbors, receiving from them reproaches and vexation as a cure for our spiritual wounds, while reproaching ourselves for impatience, but not them; instead we must thank them, for through them we came to know our spiritual infirmity, by God's Providence. And having serenity, by God's grace, be careful not to be carried away with a high opinion of yourself, so that you again do not suffer: the enemies do not sleep, they only fear humility.

St. Macarius

SELFISHNESS

The root of all evil: selfishness and stubbornness, mixed with envy and seasoned with delusion of the enemy. Therefore one must in every way strive to extract this evil root: with humility and obedience, imitating the Lord Himself, Who humbled Himself to the form of a servant, and was obedient unto crucifixion and death on the cross.

St. Ambrose

SELF-REPROACH

Strive in every way to acquire self-reproach and humility, and be attentive and watch over the movements of your heart.

St. Macarius

Watchfulness over yourself and self-reproach at all times produce humility, and that preserves peace.

St. Macarius

How do you reproach yourself? Very simply. The conscience immediately speaks out, it immediately censures us, and we have only to agree that we acted wrongly and humbly turn to God with a prayer for forgiveness. Even if only for a minute, you must absolutely reproach yourself in this way. Our job is to reproach ourselves, even if it is just for a brief time, and the rest is up to God.

St. Barsanuphius

When we reproach ourselves we use our strength and we become stronger—spiritually, of course. Why this is, we do not know. This is a law of spiritual life. Just as in our physical life we are strengthened by food, so also in the spiritual life our spiritual powers are strengthened by self-reproach.

St. Barsanuphius

If we happen to be reproached or scorned by someone, we must instruct our heart to say: "We're worse than they are,"—not only with the tongue but with a heartfelt pledge.

St. Macarius

For whatever you are guilty of before God and man, offer repentance and humble yourself, do not dare to condemn or judge anyone, but in every unpleasant situation strive to lay the blame on yourself and not others, either for your sins or that you caused this sorrow—through carelessness and inexperience.

St. Ambrose

Consider everyone to be better than yourself, and reproach and scold yourself in every way, and do not be ashamed to bow down and ask forgiveness from your neighbor for your weakness when you have something against him. Consider every day as possibly your last and, in your thoughts, place yourself more often at the judgement of God. In your heart unceasingly say the prayer: "Lord Jesus Christ, through the Theotokos have mercy on me a sinner."

St. Ambrose

No matter who he might be, always consider him to be better than you, and as you gradually get used to this you will regard everyone as an angel, and you yourself will be at peace. But as long as your self-loving part is not subdued, much fire will be required to burn it up.

St. Macarius

The Lord hears the prayers of everyone. Only those of the proud does He not accept. But He always accepts the prayers of the humble and those who reproach themselves. The Lord helps us. He cannot abandon us, for He loves us.

St. Anatoly

When they reproach you, if you can endure it— endure it; if you cannot—answer quietly.

St. Anatoly

Just as a person does not notice how he grows, how from a small infant he becomes an adult, so also the spiritual growth of a person occurs completely unnoticed by him. This is the unseen spiritual growth of a person and it consists of self-reproach.

St. Barsanuphius

Reproach yourself. To reproach yourself is not difficult, but some do not want to do it. To endure a reproach from a brother is more difficult, but to reproach yourself is not hard. However, if we do reproach ourselves but do not battle with the passions, and we eat as much as we want and sleep as much as we want, such self-reproach is not lawful and will bring no benefit.

St. Barsanuphius

When the devil points out to you the faults and weaknesses of others and urges you to judge them, then you say to yourself: "I am worse than everyone else, I deserve eternal torments. Lord have mercy on me." And even if you say this without feeling, you still need to say it.

St. Barsanuphius

SELF-WILL

It is impossible, in a short time, to acquire the habit of cutting off our will in word alone without the shedding of blood, i.e., without labors, since our previous life until now has passed in self-will.

St. Anthony

By desiring to live or die in this place, but not that one, we establish our own will, we desire to fulfill our own desires, which we must not do. Do not pray to the Lord for any such thing, but pray that His holy will may be fulfilled in us.

St. Hilarion

If you sincerely desire to have freedom from the passions and from all spiritual ailments and blasphemous thoughts, and learn humility, you must spit out all your rebellious pride and trample it with your own feet. Through this your youth will be renewed as an eagle, and from a self-willed and sinful man you will be made an Angel of God, or at least smaller than the smallest of the angels, i.e., without wings.

St. Anthony

For a young man to have his own way is harmful to the soul, and the effects are even more destructive.

St. Leo

Since you have acknowledged your negligence and laziness in not fulfilling your prayer rule, may the Lord forgive you, and I the unworthy one forgive you and I advise that you start living not according to your own will, but according to the Divine Commandments and the advice of whomever you turn to with faith. But, in living according to your own will, although it seems that you sow a great deal, the harvest is futile—flee from this.

St. Leo

Arbitrariness leads to vainglory and ends in spiritual harm, but when the same deed is performed with a blessing, then for the sake of the prayers of the brethren and the superior the Lord protects the novice from everything harmful and he receives spiritual benefit.

St. Moses

FAMILY LIFE

For a woman, marriage is service to the Most Holy Trinity—see what a great honor it is to be a wife and a mother.

St. Nektary

Happiness in married life is granted only to those who fulfill the Divine Commandments and treat marriage as a Mystery of the Christian Church.

St. Nektary

Those who enter into marriage due to the attraction of the passions are most often unhappy in life.

St. Joseph

Married life is a life blessed by God, and monastic life is a holy and angelic life; both of these ways of life are pleasing to God.

St. Anthony

We must consider not marriage, but adultery to be vile, filthy, cursed and offensive to God, His Angels, and pious people. Adultery must be abhorred as a great abomination before men. It is better to agree to die a hundred deaths than to defile yourself with such a foul vice and anger God and be deprived of His Heavenly Kingdom. Therefore, all of us, both men and women, at gatherings must avoid amorous and adulterous glances, double entendres, bold movements of the body, and immodest attire, but we must at all times maintain modesty and good Christian propriety.

St. Anthony

THE HEART

Follow the movement of your heart and vanquish those passions which arise, but mainly pride, anger, wrath, judgement, and condemnation of your neighbors. How can we weep for other deceased people when our corpse lies before us—our soul deadened by sins?

St. Macarius

Do not allow your heart to become attached to the corruptible goods of this world, but drive from it every passion, because only in a free heart, free from all passion, can the Lord make His abode.

St. Barsanuphius

Purity of heart is achieved through keeping the Divine Commandments, without which the spiritual life in general is meaningless. The battle with the passions and cleansing the heart of the passions is essential. Humility is indispensable as an unshakable foundation.

St. Nikon

With a sincere confession, the Jesus Prayer, and fulfillment of the Divine Commandments, attentively strive to cleanse your heart from everything displeasing to God.

St. Nikon

SORROWS

Do not be despondent because of the sorrows of this life; this is our lot, this is the judgement of God.

St. Nikon

It is impossible to pass your entire life without temptations and sorrows, and to always be happy and without a care. Know that God is caring for you when He sends sorrows and griefs, and with them He tries to instruct you and make you more wise in spiritual understanding. Without sorrows we cannot be humble or acquire spiritual understanding. And be assured that without God's permission, no kind of sorrow can come to us. Although it may seem that people are the cause of them, they are the instruments by which God acts in the work of our salvation.

St. Macarius

If God sends someone sorrows, it is in order to cleanse him of sins and prepare him for the eternal Kingdom of Heaven. Here everything is temporal, but there it is eternal.

St. Macarius

Accept sorrows with thanksgiving and self-reproach, and the Lord will help you and forgive you all your sins.

St. Leo

You will never flee from sorrows for they are a product of your own passions, for exposing them, so that, with God's help, we might take care to heal them.

St. Macarius

If you want to find consolation amid sorrows, with your heart quickly turn to the Lord, the One Comforter. Try yourself, according to the word of God, i.e., repent, correct yourself, believe in Jesus Christ with your heart and soul and flee to Him, as your only Savior. The more you pray to God in time of sorrow, the sooner you will feel sweet consolation.

St. Anthony

That life goes on not without sorrow—what can you do? For there has never been a person on earth so fortunate that has spent his whole life without sorrows and without tears, since we live not in the Kingdom of Heaven but in the valley of tears. But there is hope that they who sow with tears will reap with joy. Therefore cast your sorrows on the Lord and He will nourish you.

St. Anthony

Your task is to perceive the goodness and love of God for you in this temporary punishment that has befallen you. For by temporary sorrows the Most Merciful Lord wishes to deliver us from the most horrible eternal torments, which are terrifying even to think of. Therefore, with the righteous Job cry out to the Lord: *Blessed be the name of the Lord from now unto the ages!* (cf. Job 1:21)

St. Joseph

Labor according to your conscience, pray to God and ask for patience. Sorrows are a good sign. They show that we are on the narrow path. Humble yourself more and reproach yourself.

St. Joseph

Do not be disturbed and do not fear sorrows. Sorrows and joys are closely connected to each other, so that joy brings sorrow, and sorrow—joy. To you this seems strange, but remember the words of the Savior: A *woman when she is in travail hath sorrow, because her hour is come: but as soon as she is delivered of the child, she remembereth no more the anguish, for joy that a man is born into the world* (John 16:21). Day changes to night, night to day, foul weather to fine weather. Likewise sorrow and joy succeed each other.

St. Barsanuphius

Sorrows lead to heaven: thus it has been established by God, for the cleansing of sins, so as not to allow more serious sins, and for receiving the eternally joyous and blessed life in heaven.

St. Joseph

The Kingdom of Heaven is not granted to those who lie in bed, but only to those who labor and endure sorrows.

St. Joseph

He who turns to God with his whole heart and prays to Him often will escape many sorrows, and if we do not desire voluntary labors, then we must endure involuntary sorrows, in order to be with the saints. It was said: "Nothing defiled may enter the Kingdom of heaven." This means that whoever wishes to enter this Kingdom absolutely must suffer grief.

St. Anatoly

In saving us, God has established that no one can avoid sorrows, because the Lord wants everyone to be saved, and without sorrows it is impossible to be saved. In sorrows is concealed the mercy of God! This is what the holy fathers teach. Endure, and you will be saved.

St. Anatoly

By necessity you must endure the insults, for you must endure something for your sins, if not here, then in the future life. Only in the future life the sorrows are extremely horrible. May the Lord deliver us from them, through His grace and love for man.

St. Joseph

If we will not endure sorrows, and if we do endure them, but with complaining, anger, vexation, and irritation, what kind of patience is that? This is merely planting malice and anger in yourself, from which you will get pride. It is not surprising at all that a monk endures sorrows which the world does not even know. The path to the Heavenly Kingdom is narrow and thorny; the first to travel this path was the Savior of the world Himself.

St. Joseph

You need not be despondent. Let those be despondent who do not believe in God. For them sorrow is burdensome, of course, because besides earthly enjoyment they have nothing. But believers must not be despondent, for through sorrows they receive the right of sonship, without which it is impossible to enter the Kingdom of Heaven.

St. Barsanuphius

The power of suffering is not in the magnitude of the sufferings themselves, but in how a person bears them. Sometimes seemingly insignificant circumstances cause a person the greatest sorrow. One must sympathize. One and the same fact can cause suffering of various degrees in various people. This depends on how a person accepts them.

St. Nikon

Continuous sorrows sent to a person by God are a sign of especial Divine Providence for the person. The meaning of sorrows is greatly diverse: they are sent either to stem evil, or for teaching, or for more glory. For instance, a person becomes sick and he grieves over this, but at the same time, through this illness he is being delivered from a greater evil which he had intended to do.

St. Barsanuphius

If sorrows surround you—rejoice, for then you are traveling on the right path. And he who does not run away from sorrows, but bears them as he is able, will receive the Eternal Kingdom.

St. Anatoly

If you want to rejoice with ineffable joy, then endure those sorrows which are sent to you from God, and you will not regret it.

St. Anatoly

Do not look for sorrows yourself, which you are not obliged to seek, but seek, and seek diligently, Him Whom we are absolutely obliged to seek: Jesus, our Bridegroom, our Nourisher, our Hope, the Life and Light of our eyes! And we will not be ashamed.

St. Anatoly

In order for one to bear sufferings more easily, one must have strong faith, fervent love for the Lord, not be attached to anything earthly, and completely submit to the will of God.

St. Nikon

In time of sorrows and temptations the Lord helps us. He does not free us from them, but grants us the strength to endure them easily, and even not notice them.

St. Nikon

The Lord desires that we humble ourselves and imitate Him, the Humble and Meek, and that, like Him, we bear our sorrows, even though they are not like the ones He bore for our sins, but small, and a thousand times less. But we do not at all want what God wants, but insist on having our way—even though it is worse.

St. Anatoly

In order that sorrow not oppress us excruciatingly, we must reject our own will and humble ourselves before God in all aspects. God desires our salvation and He inscrutably arranges it for us. Submit to the will of God and you will find peace for your sorrowing heart and soul.

St. Nikon

When sorrows shake our souls, our hearts tremble, and our thoughts are confused, our only refuge is the Lord.

St. Nikon

It is imperative that our faith and every good work be tried. This trial is accomplished through sorrows.

St. Nikon

Let us endure for a little while and we will receive eternal blessedness. Let us consign to oblivion all earthly pleasures and joys—they are not for us. It has been said: Where our treasure is, there our heart will be (cf. Luke 12:34), and our treasure is in heaven; therefore let us strive with all our heart for the heavenly Fatherland. There all our sorrows will be turned to joy; abuse and disparagement—to glory; sorrows, tears and sighs—to consolation; sicknesses and toil—to everlasting peace without pain.

St. Hilarion

In our sorrows, people are merely the instruments, but they have no power over us. And so, let us endure everything.

St. Nikon

Sorrows are only like the rod of a father, raised in love over his unruly children in order to correct them and keep them well-behaved, which will benefit them throughout their life. Divine Providence is administered for the benefit of our souls, in order to save them in the future life.

St. Leo

Forget about impossible dreams, excessive ascetical feats and exalted ways of life, and let us begin with humility by enduring sorrows. When our souls are prepared, and if it is the will of God, it will be given to us to proceed higher.

St. Nikon

Sorrows are allowed so that it will be revealed who really loves God. Without enduring sorrows, even a grateful soul is not fit for the Kingdom of God. The steadfast endurance of sorrows is equal to martyrdom. Sorrows are insignificant in comparison to spiritual blessings.

St. Nikon

When sorrow comes to us, we must await consolations, but after the consolation, we must again await sorrows.

St. Hilarion

We cannot live in such a way that no one grieves or offends us, for the Apostle Luke writes: *we must through much tribulation enter into the kingdom of God* (Acts 14:22), and *bear ye one another's burdens, and so fulfill the law of Christ* (Gal. 6:2).

Let us therefore ask that we may bear sorrows with self-reproach and humility and not be overcome by evil, but overcome evil with good, and with the Prophet say: *With them that hate peace I was peaceable* (Ps. 119:6).

St. Hilarion

When there are sorrows and you do not have the strength to endure them, then turn with all your heart to the Lord, the Mother of God, St. Nicholas, the saint whose name you bear, and the sorrow will be alleviated.

St. Nektary

Error and delusion in man come from the fact that we do not properly understand the purpose and will of God concerning ourselves. According to His goodness and mercy, the Lord wants to give us eternal blessedness in heaven, in the Heavenly Kingdom, but we, in our blindness seek and are more desirous of temporal happiness and well-being on earth. So the Lord, in His goodness and love for the human race, instructs us with various sorrows, sicknesses, and other misfortunes.

St. Ambrose

One thing is the judgement of God, another is that of man. Concerning things near to our heart we often judge according to our passions which war against us, or we judge in opposition to ourselves, and therefore our judgement is often distorted, and what seems to us to be distressing and grievous at the present time, later is joyful, light and blessed. The end crowns the work.

St. Nikon

If the sun shines all the time, then everything in the field withers; therefore rain is needed. If it rains all the time, then everything rots, because wind is needed to aerate everything. And if there is insufficient wind, then a storm is needed to wash everything away. In a person, everything happens beneficially at its proper time because he is changeable.

St. Ambrose

A continuously happy life produces extremely unhappy consequences. In nature we see that there are not always pleasant springs and fruitful summers, and sometimes autumn is rainy and winter cold and snowy, and there is flooding and wind and storms, and moreover the crops fail and there are famine, troubles, sicknesses and many other misfortunes. All of this is beneficial so that man might learn through prudence, patience and humility. For the most part, in times of plenty he forgets himself, but in times of various sorrows he becomes more attentive to his salvation.

St. Ambrose

If a person endures sorrows with submission to the will of God, while confessing his sins, through this he will be delivered from the threat of eternal torments. Therefore, it is better to endure troubles here, no matter how difficult they may be, casting your sorrow upon the Lord and praying to Him with humility, that He deliver us from faintheartedness and despair, which are worse than any other sins.

St. Ambrose

Woe to our times: we now depart from the narrow and sorrowful path leading to eternal life and we seek a happy and peaceful path. But the merciful Lord leads many people from this path, against their will, and places them on the sorrowful one. Through unwanted sorrows and illnesses we draw closer to the Lord, for they humble us by constraint, and humility, when we acquire it, can save us even without works, according to St. Isaac the Syrian.

St. Macarius

When you see that you are depressed, do not forget to reproach yourself. Recall how much you are guilty of before the Lord and before yourself, and admit that you are not deserving of anything better—and you will immediately feel relief.

St. Ambrose

Boredom is the grandfather of despondency, and laziness is the daughter. In order to drive it away, exert yourself at work, do not be lazy at prayer; then boredom will pass and zeal will come. And if you add patience and humility to this, you will spare yourself from much evil.

St. Ambrose

I advise you to cheer up with prayer, even if it is brief, and the trust that just as after winter and severe bad weather pleasant springtime arrives, so also after boredom pleasant delights quickly appear; and therefore console yourself with this hope.

St Anthony

Boredom—just to look at something. Why is this? Because inside it is all rotten. What is the cure? Endure. Outside are the young birches: how terrifying it was for them during the autumn winds and the winter blizzards, but now look how the little buds are shooting out—they are really rejoicing. And so with us: as much as we endure, that much will we rejoice.

St. Anatoly

You are bored because you think too much about yourself and you censure those who are weak.

St. Hilarion

TEARS

Do not believe those tears that flow before you have completely cleansed yourself of all your sins.

St. Leo

TENDING THE SICK

Tending the sick is one of the most powerful means of preserving purity.

St. Macarius

DEATH

You must not be greatly troubled about many things, but you should care for the main thing—preparing yourself for death.

St. Ambrose

It is better to use your leisure time by reflecting on the sins committed during your youth and in ignorance, and on the painful repentance and confession of them, by occupying yourself more often with prayer, even if it is brief, by communing of the Holy Mysteries, even if once a month, and by thinking: "Woe is me a sinner, woe, not having any good deeds! How will I appear before the Divine Judgement? How can I dwell with the saints?"

St. Anthony

There is nothing nearer to us than death! And wherever you may end your life with hope in the salvation of God and will be lowered into the grave, everywhere the earth is the Lord's!

St. Anthony

We all now live and walk in the shadow of death, for death is not across the seas, but is right behind each of us. We become afraid because of the death of this one or that one, but the thought of correction we put off for the future, when our tongue will not be able to speak.

St. Anthony

In whatever place a person is determined by the Lord to die, even if it be abroad and thousands of miles away, he will unfailingly be at his determined place and at his time, for the commandment of God is fulfilled exactly.

St. Anthony

We cannot ascertain why a young man dies prematurely, while another elderly man yearns for it his whole life, and groans from work and exhaustion but does not die. The Lord God arranges and grants what is beneficial for each of us, most wisely, lovingly and inscrutably.

St. Anthony

In the depths of His wisdom and love for man the Lord God arranges everything and grants to everyone what is profitable, i.e., if someone's life is extended, he does good in that time; and if someone's days are shortened, it is so that evil does not change his understanding or flattery deceive his soul. Thus does the Lord God arrange everything with true love for man, and He grants unto all what is profitable. But our duty, in either situation, is to say to the Heavenly Father with childlike submissiveness: "Our Father, may Thy will be done!"

St. Anthony

How good it is to meet death with prayer! But for this you have to get used to it, while you are healthy.

St. Nikon

Fear of death is from the demons. They strike such fear in the heart that it loses hope in the mercy of God.

St. Nikon

The Lord is long-suffering. He ends the life of a man only when He sees that he is ready to pass on to eternity or when He sees that there is no hope for his correction.

St. Ambrose

LAUGHTER

Laughter drives away the fear of God.

St. Ambrose

She was bold and audacious from laughter—the fear of God began to diminish.

St. Ambrose

HUMILITY

It is not when we are considered to be humble, when we merely belittle ourselves, but when we are belittled by others and we are not disturbed by it, that we are worthy of the name. Also, our spiritual barrenness should be enough to bring us to the depths of humility, and the passions which torment us should likewise produce this action.

St. Macarius

You should look downward. Remember: you are earth and you will return to the earth.

St. Ambrose

Vainglory comes from a lack of humility. No sorrows will overcome a humble man. He does not fall, for by humbling himself he finds that because of his sins he is deserving of even more punishment. A humble man is like the man who built his house on a rock: *And the rain descended, and the floods came, and the winds blew, and beat upon that house; and it fell not; for it was founded upon a rock* (Matt: 7:25).

St. Barsanuphius

Humility is the invisible weapon against all the snares of the enemy, but acquiring it is not without difficulty, and it is even beyond the grasp of those living in the world.

Even though you reproach yourself in word, do not put your faith in that, until you have acquired true and sincere humility.

St. Macarius

Our impatience before our elders shows our weakness and lack of humility, which we still have not reached and are far away from...

St. Leo

Strive so that inner humility agrees with your outward acts of humility. Consider yourself the worst and least of all, not just by saying it, but securing the thought in your heart; it will bring you peace.

St. Macarius

It is essential that every action be mixed with humility; whether you are praying, or fasting, turning away from the world, or fulfilling an obedience—do everything for the sake of God and do not think that you are doing something good.

St.Macarius

The foundation of monastic life is humility. If there is humility, there is everything, but if there is no humility, there is nothing. With only humility one can be saved, even without any works.

St. Barsanuphius

Let the following be for you signs of humility or pride: the latter scorns everyone, reproaches them, and sees darkness in them, while the former sees only his own faults and does not dare to judge anyone.

St. Macarius

Repent, humble yourself, submit to the sisters in whatever you can, and do not condemn others; everyone has her infirmities.

St. Ambrose

Acknowledging your sinfulness, acquire humility which greatly intercedes before the Lord, both for the forgiveness of sins and for upholding us in the future, in fulfilling His commandments.

St. Macarius

Humble people are not annoyed with anyone either in spirit or in thought, but always consider themselves to be guilty and sinful, and they do not complain about anyone but they thank God for everything.

St. Anthony

A humble person lives on earth as if in the Kingdom of Heaven, always happy, peaceful, and satisfied with everything.

St. Anthony

God visits with His mercy only the humble.

St. Ambrose

Humble yourself in spirit more—humility takes the place of works. Endure all misfortunes and entrust yourself to the Lord.

St. Ambrose

Truly lamentable is that person who does not have humility. He who is not able to humble himself will later on be humbled by other people. And he whom other people cannot humble, God will humble.

St. Anthony

May the Lord help us acquire our much longed-for humility through the recognition of our infirmities.

St. Macarius

When you think of yourself as nothing, what does it matter what they think or say about you? A humble person is always calm and peaceful, but until we acquire this many trials are needed. In every situation in which you are agitated, admit your weakness and reproach yourself, but not others.

St. Macarius

The Lord arranges everything for our spiritual benefit. For how could we be humbled if we continually felt spiritual consolation? So the Lord withdraws from us so that we see our infirmity and spiritual nakedness.

St. Joseph

Pray to God for the one who abuses you and consider her your benefactor and do not in any way take revenge. Of course the enemy is urging her to do this—you should hate the enemy, but love her and pray to God for her. In this you will learn humility, when the younger ones reproach you. And consider yourself deserving of this, because of your sins.

St. Joseph

In your weaknesses and the falls which occur humble yourself, not only with your tongue, but with sincere feeling, that you may receive a token of a good work.

St. Macarius

By all means strive to acquire the opposite of pride—humility; and how it is acquired you will learn in the books of the holy fathers: continual self-reproach is the shortest path to it.

St. Macarius

It is essential to humble oneself. Without humility, virtue, and in general nothing, will bring any kind of benefit.

St. Barsanuphius

Two virtues —love and humility —depend so much on each other, just like warmth and light.

St. Barsanuphius

Acknowledge your sinfulness in your pride and impatience and humble yourself under the strong hand of God, accusing no one but yourself, and then you will see Divine help: how God will calm you and cause the hearts of those who oppose you to be favourably disposed towards you.

St. Macarius

Why is there no peace in our bones, in our soul and in our heart? Because of our sins! Because we are not at all instructed in humility, because we very much love to argue and prove that we know more than others, because we do not stop conversing with our thoughts, which along with sorrows continually torment us.

St. Anthony

Be peaceful, strong, and courageous in your spiritual battles, and not fainthearted. A powerful weapon against the enemy is self-reproach and humility, and therefore it is difficult. It destroys all of his powers and he opposes it: experience will demonstrate its benefit.

St. Macarius

Strive more to humble yourself. Humility covers all faults and forgives sins.

St. Joseph

Pride loves to have the advantage over everyone, but humility compares itself with no one, considering itself worse than all.

St. Anthony

All evil proceeds from pride, but all good is obtained with humility. This is a great virtue—humility! And like a precious stone it is rarely found, but especially in the present disastrous time.

St. Macarius

Do not be proud and vainglorious, neither by yourself nor before others. It has been said: *Do not sound the trumpet before thee and before others* (Matt. 6:2), but consider yourself worse than all others and get used to the thought that you have been sentenced to the torments of hell, that you are deserving of them, and that you can be delivered from them only by the mercy of God. This is not easy, however, and only the saints reach the stature of considering themselves worthy of torments of hell and considering themselves worse than everyone.

St. Barsanuphius

Humble yourself more in thought before God and men, and in this way you will see the Kingdom of God within yourself, and at that time your face will radiate with fervent peace and a pleasant smile.

St. Anthony

When coldness and distraction come you must not be disturbed by this, but at that time you must reproach yourself more before the Lord and humble yourself, considering yourself more sinful than all other people.

St. Joseph

In order to enter the Kingdom you must first of all be humble. How do you receive humility? How do you learn this great art? We must implore the Lord to bestow this gift on us. In one of the evening prayers we read: "Lord, grant me humility, chastity and obedience."

St. Barsanuphius

One can acquire humility by means of obedience. The person who submits his will to his spiritual guide overcomes pride and acquires humility.

St. Barsanuphius

Without humility one cannot be a disciple of Christ. Without humility the heart of a man does not receive, does not assimilate the teachings of Christ. Humility inspires the heart of a man to be submissive to the will of God, to humbly accept everything that the Lord is pleased to send on his path of life, to submit his mind, his understanding, and his desires in obedience to Christ.

St. Nikon

Humble yourself before God. Humble yourself as much as you can also before people. Do not scorn anyone. When you are at fault—immediately repent: Lord forgive! Lord have mercy! Lord help me!

St. Anatoly

Everything is all right if we reproach and humble ourselves. However, many are trying to climb up to heaven, piling ascetical struggles on themselves, but they do not want to humble themselves. Humble yourself, humble yourself!

St. Barsanuphius

Humble yourself, humble yourself. All science, all the wisdom of life are summed up in these words: *I was brought low and the Lord saved me* (Ps. 114:5). Humble yourself and endure everything. Learn humility and patience and you will have peace of soul. Be assured, that for one who has peace of soul, even prison camp will be like Paradise.

St. Barsanuphius

The most important thing—humble yourself. As soon as you lose humility and self-reproach—beg forgiveness.

St. Anatoly

If someone offends you, don't tell anyone about it except your elder, and you will be peaceful. Bow to everyone, paying no attention whether they respond to your bow or not. You must humble yourself before everyone and consider yourself the worst of all. If we have not committed the sins that others have, perhaps this is because we did not have the opportunity—the situation and circumstances were different. In each person there is something good and something bad; we usually see only the vices in people and we see nothing that is good.

St. Ambrose

Humility—this is something great and divine, and the path to it is to consider yourself below everyone. What does this mean, to consider yourself below everyone? To not notice the sins of others. Look at your own sins. Pray unceasingly.

St. Nikon

Strive to humble yourself with all your powers. And the thought that they do not love you is purely demonic. We are obliged to love everyone, but we do not dare demand that they love us.

St. Anatoly

Even though you are sinful, be humble, and you will be at peace. It is the humble that the Lord regards.

St. Anatoly

For us who seek salvation, what is most needed in fulfilling the Divine commandments is humility, which attracts to us Divine Grace and illumines all our actions. But without it no ascetical struggles and labors can bring us much desired peace.

St. Leo

Where humility does not dwell, there disdain and arrogance abide.

St. Leo

Do not be despondent because you are not living as you should, but humble yourself and the Lord will look more favorably on your humility than on struggles which are great but not humble.

St. Anatoly

Without humility you cannot be saved. Whatever structure of virtues you might build, it will collapse without humility.

St. Nikon

Abandon that deceptive thought that in some far away place you will humble yourself and will bear every disparagement and humiliation, but rather humble yourself at the present time and in the present place where you live, and in your thoughts consider yourself beneath the feet of everyone, i.e., consider yourself worthy of every disparagement, humiliation, and vexation.

St. Ambrose

Forgiveness is learned only by him who considers himself to be guilty. Humble yourself before God and people, and the Lord will never leave you.

St. Nikon

Humbly considering ourselves, until our very death, capable of every sin, from the smallest to the greatest (according to our understanding), we must fervently pray to the Lord for help, "that we enter not into temptation." Conceit takes no care in safe-guarding itself and is the cause for great falls; temptations lift a man to the heights and then cast him down.

St. Nikon

You ask: "By what path do I go to God?" Go on the path of humility! By humbly bearing the difficult circumstances of life, by humbly enduring sicknesses sent by the Lord, by the humble hope that you will not be abandoned by the Lord, the quick Helper and Heavenly Father overflowing in love, by humble prayer for help from on high to dispel despondency and feelings of helplessness by which the enemy of salvation tries to bring us to despair, which is so perilous for man, depriving him of Divine Grace and removing from him the mercy of God.

St. Nektary

When your heart is troubled keep silent, but not with anger. If you see that angry thoughts are secretly acting in you, depart and pray to God for those who have grieved you and ask for mercy through their prayers. Always try to find the fault in yourself, and if this time you were not at fault, then the reproach is being sent for previous sins and to expose our woeful condition.

St. Leo

We must view ourselves humbly and think soberly. Where there is humility, salvation is not far away!

St. Leo

If they catch on to you firmly, say to yourself: "you're not a cotton print; you will not run."

St. Ambrose

Humility consists in yielding to others and considering yourself worse than all. This way will be much more peaceful.

St. Ambrose

He who yields obtains more.

St Ambrose

Humble yourself and all your affairs will proceed.

St. Ambrose

Walk on the path of the publican and you will be saved--say: *God, be merciful to me a sinner!* (Luke 18:13)

St. Ambrose

Let us be peaceful and quiet, and even more humble. Then everything will be for our benefit according to Scripture: *Unto the pure all things are pure* (Titus 1:15). Let everything be for us spotlessly clean.

St. Ambrose

Humility consists in not judging and not reproaching anyone, and having simple clothing and furniture in your cell.

St. Ambrose

Do not look for any kind of gifts, but rather strive to acquire the mother of all gifts —humility —that is more enduring.

St. Ambrose

The humble do not investigate the depth of the unknown, but they humble their thinking, and in time God enlightens them.

St. Macarius

In the case of some sort of fall in deed, word, or thought, it is imperative to repent immediately, and acknowledging your infirmity, humble yourself and force yourself to see your sins, but not your correction. From examination of his sins a person comes to humility and he acquires a heart broken and humbled which God will not despise.

St. Hilarion

In reading the teaching of the holy fathers, do not soar aloft, but, seeing your weakness, descend to the depths of humility. It alone can save us, and without it all of our works and virtues will bring no benefit.

St. Macarius

CONFUSION

In confusion there is no benefit, but the greatest harm: It is the chariot of the enemy and it does not allow one to pour out his heart before God with repentance.

St. Macarius

Confusion, whatever kind it may be, is a sign of hidden pride and indicates the inexperience and unskillfulness of a person in the performance of his work.

St. Ambrose

In seeing your faintheartedness, recognize also where it comes from: obviously, from self-love, which cannot bear insults—it becomes confused.

St. Macarius

Consider, what kind of benefit is there from confusion after some sort of fall? Wouldn't it better to humble yourself and offer up repentance? In this peace is born, but there they are deprived of it.

St. Macarius

Humility brings peace and gives a certainty of correction, but confusion further aggravates the situation and the enemy raises a greater battle against us.

St. Macarius

The main cause of confusion is scorn of one's neighbor and lack of self-reproach, and the enemy has the power to raise up an even greater storm of confusion when we are in such a state.

St. Macarius

In every situation confusion is from the devil, from whom may the Lord shield and protect us.

St. Leo

UNION WITH GOD

The entrance of the Lord into the soul of a person is prepared by expelling from it every sin.

St. Nikon

In order for our heart to be ready and capable of receiving the call from God, it is essential to purify it of every evil, so that there is no kind of malice in it, no kind of passion for anything, and especially for anything sinful.

St. Nikon

Just as in ancient times the Lord called His disciples, so now He does not cease to call each of us to Himself. But our souls have become extremely hardened and attached to the earth, and we do not hear the voice of the Lord. We remain and stay in our unrepentant condition.

St. Nikon

If we will be with Christ and in Christ, then no kind of sorrow will confuse us, but joy will fill our heart so that even in times of sorrows and temptations we will rejoice.

St.Nikon

If we will always be with the Lord then we will have the power and might to bear witness of Him, and we will have the courage, firmness, and strength to confess Him, and confess not only with the tongue, but with our very life.

St. Nikon

Every person is a house of God. He is destined to be a dwelling of the Holy Spirit so that in him there might be offered unceasing doxology to God. But God can abide only in a pure heart; one must prepare a place for Him. How to do this? We purify ourselves of the passions and pray. Then our heart will be a temple—the house of God. We will then see God's care for us and we will unceasingly glorify Him.

St. Nikon

COMPUNCTION

There is true compunction when our heart groans without any kind of pride, not looking for any consolation for itself.

St. Macarius

SALVATION

Our salvation consists in faith and hope in the mercy of God, and the devotion of ourself and all of us to His holy will.

St. Macarius

One can be saved anywhere; do not renounce the Savior. Hold on fast to the robe of Christ, and He will not abandon you.

St. Barsanuphius

Without self-reproach, humility, patience, and love it is impossible to be saved; by means of these the battles are made easier and the craftiness of the enemy is overcome.

St. Macarius

How much sweat must be poured out, how many labors are needed, how many deprivations, illnesses, sorrows, sighs must be endured in order to obtain for oneself eternal rest in Heaven! But we think that lying on our pride, i.e., on a soft bed, and after a luxurious life, we will enter the Heavenly Kingdom!

St. Anatoly

Be attentive to your salvation while it is still day, i.e., you must in every way force yourself, for those who force themselves receive the Heavenly Kingdom.

St. Joseph

Save your soul —don't weave bast shoes.

St. Leo

Each of us must mainly take care for himself, for his own soul, for his personal spiritual welfare, because according to the Apostle, each of us must give an account for himself to God. Our confusion stems from the fact that we are inclined to educate others, and we try not only to persuade others, but also to dissuade, and to provide proof through various arguments.

St. Ambrose

Let us leave everything to the judgement of God, and then forget about it, worrying only about our own salvation; in doing so we can obtain spiritual peace, putting aside all of our grudges against others. If they do not do likewise, then they will have to answer for their own actions. We will be concerned about ourselves—and that will suffice us.

St. Ambrose

We are feeble. We can do nothing by our own power. No matter what great work it may be, it is all external, earthly. According to the will of God and His inscrutable judgements everything will return to nothing. Everything is temporary, and we must value it only insofar as it serves us for our salvation. We must just remember one thing, and only one thing, to care for the salvation of our soul, and leave everything else to the will of God. We must humble ourselves.

St. Nikon

ARGUMENT

One must not argue, for an argument can sometimes cause great unpleasantness. It has been said: "He is great before God who behaves humbly towards his neighbor," and "God will exalt the humble, but the proud and argumentative God will humble." One must reproach only himself for his own faults, and not his neighbor.

St. Joseph

From a person with an argumentative character, you can hardly expect anything else. In the spiritual life there is nothing worse and more harmful than argumentativeness. For a while it is sometimes concealed, but then it again is revealed in its former strength.

St. Ambrose

QUARRELS

Those who are indignant with us teach us to philosophically examine ourselves: are we really Christians? Do we love our enemies?—and to recognize in this our own infirmities.

St. Macarius

SUFFERINGS

The lot of all those who wish to be saved—is to suffer. Therefore, if we suffer, then let us rejoice, for our salvation is being carried out.

St. Nikon

PASSIONS

The passions cannot exercise dominion over us when we resist them and call on the help of God against them. Our self-love and pride strengthen the passions against us and give them victory over us.

St. Macarius

It is essential to pass beyond the borders of our passions i.e., to be completely delivered from them, and to change them into the opposite—into virtues. When we pass beyond an actual border, it is necessary to have a passport. And so, in conquering the passions we receive a new image, the passport of eternal life.

St. Barsanuphius

FEAR

You should be afraid not of cholera, but of serious sins, for the scythe of death mows a person down like grass even without cholera. Therefore, place all your hope in the Lord God, without Whose will even the birds do not die, much less a person.

St. Anthony

Fear is like a manifestation of not trusting in your own powers. Courage is like a manifestation of hope in the almighty power and help of God.

St. Nikon

FEAR OF GOD

At all times let us hold on to the fear of God, and fear of God will protect us from every evil, visible and invisible, if we immediately flee to God with repentance, and later confess this to our spiritual father.

St. Ambrose

Fear of God is acquired by fulfilling the Divine Commandments and doing everything according to one's conscience.

St. Ambrose

How does a person become bad?—from forgetting that God is over him.

St. Ambrose

HAPPINESS

A life spent with an unreproaching conscience and with humility, brings peace, tranquility, and true happiness. But wealth, honor, glory, and high rank are often the cause of many sins and make this happiness uncertain.

St. Macarius

TALENT

By talent you should understand not only riches, education, and prominence. Talents are favorable conditions for the salvation of the soul. Each of us is given talents. Poverty, sickness, various types of sorrows - these are all talents. If a person uses the talent given to him spiritually, for the salvation of his soul—he bears fruit.

St. Nikon

PATIENCE

He who endures to the end will be saved! Those who endure, it is said, will fly on wings; they will ascend like eagles. According to the Gospel, the Holy Righteous Anna was patient, sitting in the house of God until deep old age. Strive to imitate her.

St. Anatoly

From raising up the dust you won't get anything, except dust. But from patience: peace, life, and grace. You know all this will pass, just as the early morning fog dissipates as soon as the sun appears. But our sun will quickly, quickly shine. *In your patience possess ye your souls* (Luke 21:19).

St. Anatoly

We should learn patience not when we are reprimanded for a transgression, but when we are innocently reviled and reproached.

St. Macarius

With childlike submission we must endure both the pleasant and the unpleasant and give glory for everything to God Who is good, i.e., when any sorrow or sickness comes we say "Glory to Thee, O Lord!" If the sorrows and illnesses increase, again we say: " Glory to Thee, O Lord!" When the unhappy sorrows and illness have worsened and lead to the grave, again: "Glory to Thee, O Lord!"

St. Anthony

It has been determined by God that every person has some kind of cross in this life, i.e., a spiritual sorrow which he must bear undisturbedly, for there is not any benefit from faintheartedness and impatience. And since many are the tribulations of the righteous people in this life, then how much more must we sinners endure.

St. Anthony

No matter what grief you may encounter, whatever unpleasantness may happen to you, say: "I will endure this for Jesus Christ!" Just say this and it will be easier for you. For the name of Jesus Christ is powerful—with it all unpleasantness will subside, the demons will vanish; your vexation will die away and your faintheartedness will calm down when you repeat His most sweetest name. Lord! Grant me patience, courage and meekness! Lord! Grant me to see my own sins and not judge anyone!

St. Anthony

The Kingdom of God is taken by force, and without forcing oneself, no one has received it. One must bear the burdens of others, and for this implore the Lord for patience.

St. Joseph

Be patient, and in His time the Comforter will come. The Lord said: *In your patience possess ye your souls* (Luke 21:19). When you are not able and health does not permit, then entreat meekly to be excused, but mainly be patient. But when you cannot endure, reproach yourself and ask for help from God.

St. Anatoly

The one most reliable (means for) salvation—endure everything that God will send: the good and the bad.

St. Anatoly

You must be patient not only with the sorrows which befall you, but also with yourself.

St. Nikon

In order for there to be spiritual fruit, certain conditions are necessary: good seed (word) and good soil. The seed matures in the presence of patience. There are so many instances where a person, not seeing the fruit he expected, has fallen into despondency, with all his work for nothing. One must have the determination to endure everything. Only then can one hope to receive what he wishes. *In your patience possess ye your souls* (Luke 21:19).

St. Nikon

Patience is continuous good humor.

St. Nikon

We must thank the Lord for everything, the labor which He imposes on us to teach us patience, which ennobles the soul and is more beneficial for us than comfort. Evidently, this is pleasing to the Lord. Sorrows cannot befall us except through God's permission— for the sake of our sins. And these very sorrows protect us from other temptations.

St. Moses

You must gain your salvation in patience. Patience is essential. In other words—the cross is essential.

St Nikon

Sincerity and firmness of will are tested, precisely by patience and time.

St. Nikon

Believe that if it becomes difficult to endure, you are enduring by the will of God and God's righteous judgement, for the sake of your salvation.

St. Nikon

You must force yourself in order to establish discipline within yourself; you must labor in the struggle for the sake of the Lord and endure every burden and discomfort in the battle with yourself, with your passions.

St. Nikon

Grievous encounters are always difficult to bear, but we must force ourselves to bear them, according to the Apostolic teaching: *let us run with patience the race that is set before us* (Heb: 12:1), calling on the help of the Lord and praying to Him for those who have grieved us, that He may send down peace to our souls.

St. Moses

It is very sad that you are doing so poorly. Pray to God and ask Him for patience and do not despair. Do everything for God's sake, not for the sake of something temporal, and the Lord will never leave you and will not forget your labors. You must endure everyone and everyone's sorrows; without them you will not enter into peace.

St. Joseph

Have spiritual peace and have patience—with yourself and with others. Patience, according to St. Gregory the Sinaite, is stillness even within a storm.

St. Ambrose

Through unpleasant situations we recognize that we are impatient, and if impatient, it means self-loving. And recognition of this should dispose us to self-reproach and repentance, and to prayerfully ask the Lord for mercy—without unpleasant situations a person is inclined toward self-conceit.

St. Joseph

From Holy Scripture we see that sorrows bring people closer to salvation, if a person does not become fainthearted and does not despair, but arms himself with patience, along with humility and devotion to the will of God.

St. Ambrose

SOBRIETY

A dissipated life is a great spiritual tragedy. It produces an especially horrible effect on those who allow themselves this dissipation, having begun with an attentive life. A pious Christian must conduct his life with great attention to himself and sobriety. *Watch ye and pray, lest ye enter into temptation* (Mark 14:38), said the Lord.

St. Nikon

Sobriety is the path to every virtue.

St. Nikon

We must examine ourselves more deeply and carefully follow our thoughts and feelings, and weep over the passions, sinful feelings, desires and thoughts within us. We must absolutely drive them out, as being displeasing to God, and having expelled them, we must not allow them back into our hearts, for in a passionate state we cannot chant hymns to the Lord.

St. Nikon

Never place your hope in people and do not be troubled, not seeing sympathy in them; do not judge them. Attend to yourself.

St. Nikon

When you notice the faults of others and you have proud thoughts when in their presence, you must answer these demonic thoughts: "I am worse than everyone," and even if it is without feeling, you should say it nevertheless.

St. Barsanuphius

It is good that he is concerned about the inner, contemplative life, for it will give him everything.

St. Barsanuphius

Guard the eyes. *If thy right eye offend thee, pluck it out* (Matt. 5:29), the Lord has commanded. You invite a battle within yourself if you do not guard the eyes and tongue.

St. Anatoly

If someone takes part in idle talking, he cannot live attentively but is continually dissipated. From not talking silence is born; from silence—prayer, for how can one who is dissipated pray? Be attentive to yourself; the attentive life is the goal of monasticism. It is said: "Take heed to yourself!"

St. Barsanuphius

Value the time, it is irretrievable; take more heed to yourself, for your struggle consists of this.

St. Leo

VAINGLORY

Although vainglory and pride are from the same leaven and have the same nature, their actions and symptoms are different. Vainglory tries to attract the praise of men and for this it often debases itself and tries to please men, but pride exhales scorn and disrespect towards others, although it also loves praises.

St. Ambrose

To prevent vainglorious and other bad thoughts from coming is impossible; you must just battle with them and with God's help drive them away.

St. Joseph

Since every good work is entwined with vainglory and self-opinion, one must oppose it and drive it away; just as many creeping vines can choke a tree, so also vainglory destroys good works.

St. Macarius

Flee from vainglory—it corrupts all fruit.

St. Anatoly

The passion of vainglory destroys faith in the heart of man.

St. Nikon

If you touch vainglory with your finger it cries: "They are tearing the skin!"

St. Ambrose

REPROACH

For the proud, reproach is a sharp knife, but for the humble it is a valuable find.

St. Anthony

DESPONDENCY

Despondency also means laziness, only it is worse. From despondency you weaken both the body and the soul. You do not want to work or pray, you go to church with carelessness and the whole man becomes weak.

St. Ambrose

Darkness of spirit—although it is sometimes sent as a trial, still one should test: was this not sent because of pride? And one should humble himself.

St. Macarius

We should not be despondent. In the sorrows we experience is concealed the mercy of God. How the Lord arranges our life is incomprehensible for us.

St. Nikon

In times of dryness and languor we must not fall into the pit of despondency and despair, and not seek for ourselves what we are not worthy of—great Divine gifts, but find peace in humility, considering ourselves to be unworthy of them.

St. Macarius

Do not hand yourself over into the captivity of despondency and laziness, but with the brief prayer: "Lord Jesus Christ have mercy on me a sinner," repulse them.

St. Anthony

The cause of depression and fear, of course, is our sins.

St. Macarius

I offer this advice against despondency: patience, psalmody, and prayer.

St. Macarius

Some days are beautiful and joyful, and some days are dark and black due to unpleasantness of life. This shows that in joyful times we must not forget ourselves and in troubled times we must not fall in spirit, for just as foul weather is followed by pleasant weather, so too, after despondency the soul is again happy.

St. Anthony

Do not give in to despondency, but try to always be happy and content; this eases the sorrow by half.

St. Joseph

Save yourself from despondency, just like the disease of fornication. It is among the seven deadly passions.

St. Moses

When melancholy attacks you, read the Gospel.

St. Ambrose

If you are experiencing languor, then examine your conscience: is there not some unrepented sin?

St. Anatoly

HOPE IN GOD

Be brave and firm in spirit in your faith and hope in the mercies of the gracious Lord, that in the situations that seem to be opposing us He is working out our salvation. Acknowledge your weakness and your failure to submit to the will of God and to fulfill His commandments. From this acknowledgement you will obtain humility for yourself and you will see the help of God.

St. Leo

Those who labor and are heavy laden are ready for rest in the Lord. And all your labors are not worth what awaits those who labor during this brief lifetime for eternal rewards. Fight, brother, the good fight with hope in the Lord God.

St. Moses

Always hope only in God, but never in man. Then every evil will fall away from us like a branch that is lopped off.

St. Barsanuphius

Only looking to the Almighty Lord and calling out to Him will support a poor soul.

St. Moses

The common and all-evil enemy—the devil, although he makes many attacks against us, will in no way succeed as long as we hope in God.

St. Leo

Everything is possible for the Lord God—not just healing the hopelessly sick person but even raising the dead. Therefore, place all of your hope in the Lord God, with Whom there remains, both for you and for everyone, great mercy.

St. Anthony

Whoever firmly hopes in God will God help in all things.

St. Anthony

Do not worry about and do not get angry at the members of your household. You have come to God—wait on God. He is more trustworthy than all the princes and the sons of man. And do not be attracted to the present life. If you are at peace—thank God, if you are grieved—again thank God. And always await the mercy of God.

St. Anatoly

Although we must turn to men for spiritual and physical help, success in these requests we must expect from the hand of the Lord.

St. Nikon

One must never hope in man. This is a great and fatal mistake. Man will not protect or comfort unless God determines it. Man is powerless without the help of God.

St. Nikon

If we will flee to the Lord, He will visit us, enter into our heart, protect us, and shield us from every temptation. He will be for us a strong pillar in the face of the enemy and will lead us unerringly to the pinnacle of our desires and yearnings, to the eternal, blessed, Heavenly Kingdom.

St. Nikon

What good is a soldier without a battle? He is untried and uncourageous. And without battle a monk cannot acquire patience in his soul and be crowned by the Setter of the contest. Do not grow faint in spirit and do not despond during times of trouble, but turn to the Lord with humble prayer and believe that help will come to you.

St. Moses

CONSOLATION

A storm either proceeds or follows consolations, and our passionate make-up is the reason for this. Our passions are a door shutting out from us spiritual joy.

St. Macarius

The Lord is powerful enough to always console us. But continuous consolation will harm us —just as if the sun were to always shine and rain to always pour down, then everything would burn up or be trampled down. It is good that they take turns.

St. Anatoly

CHURCH

Enter into church as into the house of God. And stand in church as in the house of God, conscious of God's presence, refraining from every familiarity and lack of restraint.

St. Nikon

Visit the church of God more often. It is good to stand in some dark corner and to pray and weep for your soul. And the Lord will console you, He will certainly console you, and you will say: "Lord, I thought that there was no way out of my difficult situation, but Thou, Lord, hast helped me!"

St. Barsanuphius

Standing in Church, it is not proper to enumerate your faults, and thereby distract your attention from the reading and the chanting, but simply consider yourself a sinner because of all your sinfulness and scattered thoughts, and this is sufficient.

St. Macarius

In church, when the devil stops up your ears and closes your eyes, try to say the Jesus Prayer. Pay attention to the power of the kathismas, and they will then bring you sweetness. There is much beauty and sweetness in them which will drive away sleep and despondency.

St. Anatoly

Do not be disorderly in church, i.e., do not speak and look around, or God will allow the devil to defile your temple.

St. Anatoly

One must not speak in church. This is an evil habit. For this sorrows are sent.

St. Ambrose

The church is for us an earthly heaven where God Himself abides and looks upon those standing there. Therefore we must stand orderly in church, with great reverence. Let us love the church and let us be zealous towards it. It is a comfort and consolation for us in time of sorrows and of joys.

St. Hilarion

While standing in church one must listen attentively to the church chanting and reading, and whoever is able, must not stop saying the Prayer of Jesus, especially when the church reading is bad or incomprehensible.

St.Ambrose

To speak while standing at church services, or to look around from side to side, is not only unseemly but it angers the Lord because of our inattention and lack of fear. If we cannot do so spiritually, then at least let us physically and visibly behave ourselves properly. Physical and visible decorum can lead us to the proper inner disposition of our thoughts.

St. Ambrose

THE HEAVENLY QUEEN

Pray to the Mother of God. She will intercede for you in this life and after death she will help you to pass through the toll-houses and reach the Heavenly Kingdom.

St. Barsanuphius

THE KINGDOM OF GOD

The Kingdom of God is within you, the Lord said to us (Luke 17:21) i.e., in the heart, so it is necessary to seek it in the heart, cleansing it of the passions and provocations of the enemy, not judging or reproaching anyone.

St. Macarius

READING

Read books in the morning from the fourth hour until work, and then chew the whole day on what you have read, like a sheep with its cud.

St. Ambrose

You may copy from the books if you like, but you must assimilate it; read what is comprehensible to you. You should read less, but understand it.

St. Ambrose

What profit will books bring us if we only read them and are not roused to do anything?

St. Macarius

The comprehension of Holy Scripture is given according to the measure of our purity of heart and our humility. This depth is undiscernable and endless.

St. Macarius

Just read through the book. Even if you do not remember anything at the time (i.e., during the reading), you will receive benefit.

St. Ambrose

Read the books of the fathers and study their teaching. It will be helpful in recognizing your infirmity and in obtaining humility, patience, and love, and it enlightens us as to how to oppose the passions and cleanse our heart of thorny plants and sow the virtues.

St. Macarius

I advise you not to stop reading spiritual books, for it happens sometimes that one line, read at the right time, becomes more dear than a year of publications and remains in your memory for always.

St. Anthony

I ask you, for God's sake, to read the word of God and the instructions of the fathers more often. You will gain profit and will find there that there is only one pathway to peace—patience and humility.

St. Macarius

The best guide for you will be the reading of the Lives of the Saints.

St. Barsanuphius

THE TONGUE

If you take into consideration only your tongue, how much evil has been spoken by it—abuse against God, condemnation of neighbors, complaining, joking, blasphemy, gossip, bad language, swearing, and so on! And has one day in the year passed by in which we have not sinned with our tongue, forgetting that we will have to give account to God for every idle word? Therefore the Lord God, thinking of our correction and salvation, sends sorrows, due to which a person finds it difficult not only to take part in idle chatter, but also to speak about serious matters.

St. Anthony

Our profit comes not from the quantity of words, but from the quality. Sometimes much is said, but nothing is heard, and at another time you hear only one word and it remains in your memory for your whole life.

St. Anthony